THE IMPACT OF REFORM MOVEMENTS ON SOCIAL POLICY CHANGE:
The Case of Social Insurance

THE IMPACT OF REFORM MOVEMENTS
ON SOCIAL POLICY CHANGE:
The Case of Social Insurance

by
DANIEL S. SANDERS

Foreword by
J.F.X. PAIVA

R. E. BURDICK, Inc., Publishers
Fair Lawn, New Jersey 07410

International Standard Book Number: 0-913638-01-3
Library of Congress Catalogue Card Number: LC 73-80005

Copyright © 1973 by R. E. Burdick, Inc.,
12-01 12th Street, Fair Lawn, New Jersey 07410.
Published simultaneously in Canada by Book Center, Inc.,
1140 Beaulac Street, St.-Laurent 382, Quebec.

Printed in the United States of America.

To Christobel

Contents

Tables

Foreword

THIS BOOK IS AN EXCITING STUDY of forces that have shaped policy in the specific area of social insurance in the development of Social Security in the United States. The work is as fascinating in its scope and content as in its importance.

In the examination of the evolution of the social insurance provisions of the Social Security Act we are brought into an awareness of two different sets of factors affecting the development of social welfare in this country: on the one hand there are the strategies employed by the pressure groups and reform organizations to achieve better welfare provisions for all; on the other hand there are the forces of change over which control is not possible. More broadly, the latter constitute certain natural phenomena or central tendencies like longevity rates, the economic depression, migration, etc., which also seriously affect the course and development of social policy.

Fortunately for the reader the author has involved himself in the analysis of both these sets of factors in studying how social policy evolved. In trying to explain the behavior of reform groups, the total milieu in which other change forces were generated are also analyzed and placed before the reader in a related perspective. In so doing, the author gives the reader the benefit of a major strength in this book—a socio-economic analysis combined with a historical delineation.

This is just as well, for in the mix of the two sources of change (directed and inherent) we have a realistic picture of the ingredients that constitute the totality of change processes. It might be important to note that while social strategies consist of the conscious use of planned efforts in order to effect change, such strategies are more complete and meaningful when you also take into consideration the

irrational factors as well as the uncontrollable phenomena which impinge upon the target situation. This is more than saying that social policy has legislative and non-legislative sources.

The conclusions the author derives from his study as well as the methodology the author emplys in the analysis of the relevant variables affecting the development of social insurance are of considerable importance. Demographic factors, legislative processes, leadership roles, organizational behavior, and broad change phenomena are studied and analyzed in a manner of particular significance to the student of social policy as well as social change. For this reason the book is recommended to all those interested in learning to be agents of change.

This book will be of interest to students of social policy in particular who need to be familiar with the development of a major social policy measure in this country leading to the Social Security Act. Students from the developing countries are likely to benefit as well, especially if their countries have social insurance programs under consideration. Studies of this type fill a greatly felt need in the analysis of social policy measures and strategies.

This work is most timely in the context of the present crisis in social welfare. There are important lessons in the development of social insurance in the U.S. which this book presents to the reader for thoughtful consideration in relation to what is going on today in the field of social welfare. The author deserves the thanks of those interested in the welfare of people for this timely service.

Columbia, Missouri
February 28, 1973

J. F. X. Paiva, Ph.D.
Director, School of Social Work,
University of Missouri;
formerly of the Division of
Social Development,
United Nations Secretariat
(New York)

Preface

SOCIAL WORK AND ALLIED PROFESSIONS are increasingly addressing themselves to the task of social policy formulation and policy changes. The challenge to enter the policy arena is real, but there are considerable difficulties along the way. Several critical questions arise: What is social policy? What are the considerations in efforts at influencing social policy? To what extent could social work be viewed as a social reform movement? How realistic is it to attempt an assessment of the role of reform movements in influencing policy in a situation where the policy process seems complex, confused and a way of "muddling through"?

This book is an attempt to examine critically these and other related questions pertaining to social policy and efforts at influencing policy changes. The theoretical formulation on social policy change and the discussion on the role of the reform movements in influencing policy are based on a well documented case study of the policy changes in social insurance following the Social Security Act of 1935.

Specifically the study provides an analysis of policy changes in the amendments to the Social Security Act (social insurance policy changes) and the policy issues associated with them from 1935 to 1954.* There is also a critical appraisal of the role of key social reform movements in influencing these changes.

The reform movements studied include the labor movement, the Townsend Movement, and the women's reform movements of the day.** Social work's role in influencing policy changes in social

---

* This is roughly the period from the New Deal to the Fair Deal, the "formative years" in regard to Social Security policy and direction.
** The term "women's reform movements" here refers to organizations of women with the objectives of social reform and not to movements for women's reform.

insurance is also investigated mainly through a study of the efforts of the American Association of Social Workers (AASW), the American Public Welfare Association (APWA) and individual social workers and social reformers close to these associations.

For purposes of the study, the term "reform movements" is defined as organizations and interest groups that have the goal of bringing about specific changes in social welfare and related fields, changes in services provided or institutional changes. These are movements that attempt to effect changes within the framework of society—changes in program, changes in institutions or even changes in the distribution of power. From the point of view of strict sociological theory, associations like AASW and APWA should be viewed more as organizations with reform interests, rather than reform movements. However for purposes of this study they are included as reform movements.

The book is intended for social workers and other professional and lay persons interested in the areas of social reform, social policy, Social Security legislation and social change. It focuses on an important area of considerable current interest—social policy changes in response to changes in thought, environmental conditions and pressure of interest groups. The analysis of the policy issues and changes in social insurance and the examination of the forces that helped or hindered the growth of the social insurance movement in the United States will be of interest to other countries, particularly the "developing countries." Undoubtedly, each country will have its own unique background of historical development, thought and socioeconomic conditions, in terms of which the particular social insurance program and policy issues will be considered and policy decisions made. But this is not to deny the usefulness of learning from the experience of other countries (in this instance from the American experience), so long as there is a conscious effort made to avoid the danger of making simplistic comparisons.

This book in a real sense is due to the impetus and inspiration provided by several persons and experiences. I have also done considerable research in special libraries and archives, and have drawn

from my study and experience in the field of social policy both in the United Kingdom and the United States. There are several persons who reviewed my manuscript and made helpful suggestions and criticisms, to each one of whom I wish to express my sincere appreciation. I wish to acknowledge especially the scholarly criticisms and valuable suggestions pertaining to my study made by leaders in the field of Social Security policies whom I had the privilege to interview: Arthur J. Altmeyer, Eveline M. Burns, Clarke A. Chambers, Wilbur J. Cohen, John C. Kidneigh, Raymond Munts, Charles Schottland and Elizabeth Wickenden.

Finally my thanks go to my wife, Christobel, who typed the manuscript and whose encouragement and support made possible the writing of this book.

University of Hawaii   Daniel S. Sanders
Honolulu, Hawaii
February 1973.

I

Basic Considerations
in Policy Change Efforts

Somehow, then, if we wish improvements in security and comfort, those who better understand the problems of government and finance, of capital and labor, and of youth and of age have the task of seeing to it that needs are better provided for, that meaningful and reasonable goals are substituted for panaceas, and that a large proportion of the population does not feel that the discrepancy between its hopes and its realizations is so unbridgeable.

Hadley Cantril, *The Psychology of Social Movements* (John Wiley & Sons, Inc., © 1941.)

The Policy-Making Process

IN A DEMOCRATIC SOCIETY the policy-making process, by the very nature of the freedom and the opportunity for individual participation afforded, becomes a complex and not altogether coherent process. Policy is not handed down by any one individual or group, without any opportunity for various points of view to be heard and for different forces to interact. Policy emerges as a compromise and a solution at a given time resulting from the interaction of several forces. Policy in the real world, it is argued, "is not made once and for all; it is made and remade endlessly." Policy making is seen as a process of "successive approximation" to some "desired objectives," in which the objective desired itself is likely to change. [1]

In examining the policy-making process it is also necessary to attempt to answer the specific question: what is social policy? It has been pointed out that the term "social policy" is a lay term, used unprecisely and that it defies simple definition. Alfred Kahn refers to social policy as a British concept introduced in the United States through the writings of R. M. Titmuss, T. H. Marshall, Eveline Burns, and others. The term "social policy" as used by these authors, it is to be noted, is equivalent in meaning to "social welfare," as used in the United States. [2] Martin Rein maintains that social policy is the study of social welfare in its broadest terms. [3] He sees social policy as dealing with "multiple, vague and conflicting goals," all of which seem to be desirable and necessary. The central issue in social policy is to him "the study of social purposes and how they can be realized." [4] Social policy is seen as being concerned with varying conceptions of the purposes, principles and outcome in social welfare services; they are "a set of solutions" that tend to develop over time by "design," "accident," "compromise," or "precedent."

It is evident that the "unsettled and evolving" concept of social

policy has varying uses and interpretations. There are at least four different uses or interpretations that have been identified as follows:

1. Social policy as a philosophical concept. In an abstract sense, social policy is the principle whereby the members of large organizations and political entities collectively seek enduring solutions to . . . problems . . .
2. Social policy as a product . . . consists of the conclusions reached by persons concerned with the betterment of community conditions and social life, and with . . . amelioration . . . which lays out the intended policy . . .
3. Social policy as a process . . . the fundamental process by which enduring organizations maintain an element of stability and at the same time seek to improve conditions . . .
4. Social policy as a framework for action . . . is both product and process. It assumes the availability of a well delineated policy which is to be implemented within the context of potential changes in the values, structure, and conditions of the group affected. [5]

Needless to say, these different uses or meanings associated with social policy themselves are likely to change and are at best tentative. However, there seems to be a fair amount of agreement that at the core of social policy are choices and consideration of ends or objectives to be achieved by a course of action. Rothwell views policy in a broad sense as "a body of principles to guide action." Applied policy is seen as "a calculated choice—a decision to pursue specific goals by doing specified things." [6] There are identifiable elements such as goals, choices among conflicting values and interests, and the adoption of a particular course of action. Social policy then is to be viewed (as suggested in one study) as consisting of courses of actions pursued by the government that pertain mainly to "the social aspects of life," the kind of action "deliberately designed," and pursued "to improve the welfare of its citizens either collectively or as individuals." [7] This view of social policy is basically in agreement with the thinking of Titmuss, Marshall and

others in regard to the central focus of social policy. Marshall's view, for example, is as follows:

> Social policy, . . . is taken to refer to the policy of governments with regard to action having a direct impact on the welfare of the citizens, by providing them with services or income. [8]

The central core of this, Marshall points out, consists of areas such as public assistance, social insurance, health and welfare, housing, education and corrections.

While the focus in social policy is mainly on the intent and courses of action pursued by governments in response to specific social problems or needs, it is not limited to just governmental action. The policy-making process, especially in the social field, involves patterns of interaction between governmental and voluntary organizations, "between the official, the expert and the man in the street." Social policy in most instances is said to emerge as a compromise between diverse and conflicting values and interests; it is seen as an effort to "balance the right to freedom of action of individuals or groups with the welfare of others."

Again, the main focus on "social aspects of life" in social policy, while generally accepted, does raise the question as to whether social policy is to be confined to objectives of social welfare policies. There is a point of view that the central task of social policy relates to the objectives of social welfare policies as well as to the social aspects and objectives of economic policies. [9] It is held, for example, that social policy in such areas as Social Security and social insurance involves also examination of objectives of economic policies. Increasingly in regard to socio-economic problems such as poverty, unemployment and urban renewal, social policy may have to address itself not only to the objectives of social welfare policies, but also to the social objectives of economic policies.

It is also a misconception to think of social policy and the policy process in general as being directly responsive to human need. For the more carefully social policy is examined, the more it becomes

evident that need is only one and, at times, a minor factor and that there are other factors that come into play. [10] There are different models that influence the main purposes of social policy, such as "allocative justice," "social therapy," and the approach where policy is seen "as an instrument to achieve other goals." In allocative justice, redistribution becomes the main purpose of social policy. In social therapy the primary focus is on enabling individuals to develop a sense of belonging in their communities. Policy is seen as an instrument to promote other goals in those situations where social policy is intended, for instance, to promote economic development or social stability. [11]

The decision as to which of these models or combination of models is to be given primary emphasis itself becomes a major policy issue, particularly in the developing countries where the resource allocation is even more difficult and where everything seems to demand the highest priority. In reality social policy may well have elements of all three models, but insofar as the goals of these different models tend to be in conflict, serious consequences may arise.

There are several levels at which policy takes shape—national, state, local—and varying interest groups and value positions are represented, often in conflict with one another. There is an essential place for "moralizing" in the policy process but moralizing, it must be pointed out, should not be mistaken for policy making. Moralizing is the device for making one's value positions known. But policy making is seen as the "setting of courses of action" with a view to implementing the values, often of a large group of persons on a particular issue, without imposing the value of any one group and "without unduly compromising other values on other issues." [12]

There are conflicting goals, conflicting means, conflicting values and often conflicting interest groups that come into play in the policy process. The policy process is open-ended in regard to most fundamental issues and there is no finality in the resolving of conflicts. Policy emerges as a solution or compromise at a given time, in a given set of circumstances. It is not within the control of

any one individual or group, but rather it results from the interaction of several factors. The degree of intensity of interest varies at different times, and even the constituencies that participate in the process tend to change as time progresses.

The question has been raised in this context, if goals of social policy are contradictory and conflicting, and if factors such as differing values and interests add to the confusion, how is it possible to proceed with the task of making choices? To what extent are rational choices possible? There are two broad approaches to the policy process (and variations of these) that are referred to. There is the theoretical approach or model where the rationality of the policy process, and the possibility of rank ordering of values and priorities are assumed. Needless to say, this has been subject to the criticism that it does not fit the pattern in the real world and—the least of the criticism—that the assumption of perfect information being available is unfounded. Opposed to this rational comprehensive approach there is the more casual approach (often of "muddling through") where means and ends tend to be mixed together and there is no strict comparison of values or policies. [13]

It has been maintained that for complex problems the rational or scientific approach is not practicable since it demands extensive time, money and other resources; and that, even if these were available, it is still not possible to rely entirely on rational procedures, and the rules they offer for making choices. The question, then, is whether the scientific approach in the policy process is to be abandoned altogether? The plea is made that research or the scientific approach not be abandoned, but that its role be seen realistically. While research may seldom be in a position to contribute directly to policy formulation, it very often "provides an argument against potential critics and aids in developing specific plans." [14] Undoubtedly, reliable information and data provide a basis for policy decisions that cannot be neglected.

In every society, there are several factors that are said to determine the nature of the policy process and the kind of solutions that emerge at a given time. Among the more important of these are the

prevailing beliefs about the nature of man which, in a sense, determine the values and goals that are taken into consideration; the particular beliefs regarding the function of society and the role of government; the scientific knowledge and resources available; and the particular stage of development of each society and its level of expectation. [15] The situation is more complicated in that all of these factors interact with one another and are themselves subject to change. Furthermore, there are several actors, roles, institutions, interest groups, and value positions that come into play. [16] It is, therefore, no surprise that the study of social policy and the policy process, particularly in countries experiencing rapid social change, gives a confused picture.

There are special difficulties in determining the social policy process and the participants. Social policies are related, by and large, to people in their "consuming roles" and not to their "producing roles." The persons directly affected by social policies—the consumers, the clients—despite recent efforts are still mostly "unorganized" and "diffuse." Another feature, especially in regard to social policy, is the fact that it is often a by-product of legislation primarily aiming at other purposes. Also unintended consequences influence social policy more than deliberate efforts. [17]

Guidelines for Influencing Policy Changes

If the public policy process seems to be largely a case of "muddling through," influenced very often by situational and fortuitous factors, does it make sense to talk about possible considerations or guidelines for future efforts at making policy changes? Is there any possibility of influencing policy changes when policy emerges from the interaction of several often unpredictable forces?

However, the major components of the policy process are neither random nor fortuitous. There are "myriad decision points" in the political system, providing access to interest groups and individuals whereby policy decisions could be influenced. [18] The leaders of certain groups and associations attuned to social policy issues along

with decision makers strategically located in the political system constitute a small group referred to as the "policy system." This "policy system" is said to define the boundaries within which choices will be made but, in the final decisions, several others within the political system will have participated. [19]

The social welfare policy system, for example, includes several professional and interest groups, such as the National Association of Social Workers, American Public Welfare Association, Association of State Directors of Public Welfare, National Welfare Rights Organization, Child Welfare League, and other related groups and institutions. The components of any policy system, which in no sense is static, serve as points of reference for legislators and administrators (who are also a part of it) in policy decisions. The policy system is an indicator of the nature and intensity of agreement or disagreement in regard to a particular policy issue and whether or not it is timely to move on to action.

In this context, a basic consideration in deliberate efforts at influencing social policy changes is the realistic appraisal of the different phases in the legislative or policy process, to ascertain how effective they could be in each of these phases. Certain key elements or stages in the legislative process have been identified: the emergence of an idea, the task of organized leadership, building of political support for the proposal, the forming of alliances or negotiations between key interests, public debate and, finally, policy decisions in the legislature. [20] The order in which these different elements are presented may not always correspond to how they emerge in the policy process, but there is no serious disagreement that these are the key elements in the policy process.

Social workers and those in allied fields by the very nature of their activity and the resources at their disposal seem to have special capabilities in influencing policy at particular stages in the process. Needless to say American society is so complex and pluralistic that it is not possible for any single group or organization to succeed in introducing legislative policy changes on its own. But, aware of this realistic situation, it is still possible for social workers to utilize their

limited resources to the fullest by intervening at strategic points in the policy process.

At the heart of every major piece of social legislation, such as the Social Security Act of 1935, there is "an idea or vision" of needed changes in social, economic and political institutions. In the frequent initiation and nurture of ideas in response to need, in the vision of things to come, social workers are among those who have a unique contribution to make. This is the initial phase of the policy process: Wilbur Cohen maintains that this vision or idea is the "irreplaceable, irreducible first essential in the political process." [21] Likewise Peter Rossi points out that social workers can play a significant role "by providing ideas and issues to the politicians" and serving as "generators of ideological programs." [22] The idea as it emerges becomes controversial; there are spokesmen for and against it with equally strong feelings; and, in the "period of germination" that follows, social workers are again in a position to play an important role through their professional organizations. They are in a position to provide a "forum" for it, consider its implications and, as has been suggested, "to rework the idea into a more widely accepted policy." [23]

Here as elsewhere it is presumptuous to think that social workers by themselves can exercise a dominant role. There are undoubtedly several actors and voices, but social workers along with other strategic forces could play a more effective role. If social work is to be in a position to speak with the support of significant groups in the community, the need for greater collaborative efforts and alliances becomes imperative. One of the frequent questions addressed to representatives of NASW and other social welfare organizations who testified before congressional committees on social security changes was how representative they were. It is also evident that when social workers collaborated with the other reform movements, notably labor, the impact of their efforts at influencing Social Security changes was greater. This was evident, for example, in the success in upholding the "merit principle" in the 1939 amendments to the Social Security Act. If in the past this was attempted sporadically, it

is urgent that an ongoing and deliberate policy of collaboration and strategic alliance with other related groups be attempted in the future.

Such alliances or collaborations have to be at all levels: national, state and local; they should be "both organizational and individual." What is called for is a sustained and ongoing effort at collaboration, around related goals and particular issues. The development of such alliances has not always been easy for social workers, with their commitment to certain ethical values, priorities and goals as a profession. No one would advocate that this commitment be abandoned; but there is the need to develop the art of working with others who may not subscribe to all the profession's goals or values, but who nevertheless are important in building effective support for particular policies. In the attempt to form alliances with other groups, the goals or priority of one group "must be tempered with that of the other group." [24] This is not to belittle the goals and values that the social work profession is committed to; indeed too much is at stake if the profession abdicates its role in the area of human values.

Intimately related to policy questions is the task of rethinking some of the values that are operative in society. An obvious example is the so-called "Protestant work ethic," and the attendant tendency many times to look upon those who do not contribute to the "classical productive economy" as a "lower order of humanity." [25] While the social work profession's commitment to certain ethical values is crucial and there is a necessary place in the policy process for "moralizing," it is also important to accept realistically the difficulty, if not the impossibility, of implementing one set of values. The distinctive feature in the policy process is decision regarding the allocation of scarce resources and mediation among conflicting interests and sets of values. The policy process is always the art of the possible, and policy emerges as a compromise between conflicting values and interests.

Social work needs to develop competence to be in a position to present its value considerations and approaches to policy issues with

the support of groups with related goals, as against alternate approaches and value positions, in the hope of achieving the maximum possible. A *sine qua non* for all this is the capacity to weather storms of conflict and opposition, and to persevere till effective solutions are arrived at.

It therefore becomes clear that if the social work profession is to be in a position to influence social policy changes effectively, there is a need for greater flexibility, for changes in approaches and direction. The predominant emphasis on the individual to the relative neglect of the community and the broader environment has to be corrected. Equally important is the need to focus on the "consensus" as well as the "conflict" models in social work practice. There is also the necessity to break loose from the tendency towards being perhaps exclusively "agency- and private-power-structure-centered," and to be more "client- and community-centered." [26] In all phases of the policy process, and particularly in the "pregovernmental phase," social workers and related groups have an important contribution to make—helping to define the boundaries within which choices will be made, clarifying issues and value considerations, defining and redefining issues and helping to enlist support from a wider public.

It is said that policy makers do give attention to relevant organizations and interest groups when policy questions "germane" to the group's concerns emerge. [27] At times the controversial nature of a particular group's position may bring it into the forefront. How effective an organization is in a particular area depends on a number of factors such as organizational strength, leadership, "specificity of issue interest," and the ability to gain access to the policy process.

In the effort to form alliances with related interest groups, social workers should not overlook the client and consumer groups that could provide a wider base for movements to influence specific social policy changes. No profession has identified itself so closely with the welfare of its clients on an individual and group basis, with the constant objective of improving their capacities for social functioning. But when recipients come together to form welfare rights

organizations—in keeping with accepted principles of client participation and with the minimum possible self-determination—in efforts
to modify their environment, institutions, and policies, do professional workers tend to shy away or at best, become bewildered
spectators? This is not to deny the trend of individual social workers
toward becoming actively associated with welfare rights organizations. However, the social work profession as a whole should look
upon such client organizations as a resource, to be helped to "tell
their story" more effectively and more accurately.

NOTES

1. Charles E. Lindblom. "The Science of 'Muddling Through,'" *Readings in American Political Behavior.* Raymond E. Wolfinger, ed. Englewood Cliffs, N.J.: Prentice-Hall, Inc., 1966, p. 223.

2. See Alfred J. Kahn. *Theory and Practice of Social Planning.* New York: Russell Sage Foundation, 1969, p. 21.

3. Martin Rein. *Social Policy: Issues of Choice and Change.* New York: Random House, Inc., 1970, p. xiii.

4. *Ibid.,* Introduction, p. x.

5. Howard E. Freeman and Clarence C. Sherwood. *Social Research and Social Policy.* Englewood Cliffs, N.J.: Prentice-Hall, Inc., 1970, pp. 2-3.

6. Charles E. Rothwell, Foreword in *The Policy Sciences.* Daniel Lerner and Harold Lasswell, eds. Stanford: Stanford University Press, 1968, p. ix.

7. Joan L. M. Eyden. *Social Policy in Action.* London: Routledge and Kegan Paul, 1969, p. 5.

8. T. H. Marshall. *Social Policy.* London: Hutchinson University Library, 1967. p. 7.

9. Rein, *op. cit.,* p. 10.

10. *Ibid.,* p. 15.

11. *Ibid.,* p. 18.

12. Raymond A. Bauer and Kenneth J. Gergen, eds. *The Study of Policy Formation.* New York: The Free Press, 1968, p. 3.

13. Lindblom, *op. cit.,* pp. 211-226.

14. Rein, *op. cit.,* p. 267.

15. Eyden, *op. cit.,* p. 114.

16. Bauer and Gergen, *op. cit.,* p. 150.

17. Alan K. Campbell. "Decision-Makers in Social Policy," *The Social Welfare Forum, 1970.* New York: Columbia University Press, pp. 76-77.

18. Eugene Eidenberg and Roy D. Morey. *An Act of Congress: The Legislative Process and the Making of Education Policy.* New York: W. W. Norton & Company, Inc., 1969, p. 4.

19. *Ibid.,* p. 5.

20. Peter A. Corning. *The Evolution of Medicare, Research Report No. 29,* Office of Research and Statistics, Social Security Administration, Washington:

U.S. Govt. Printing Office, 1969, p. viii. See also Wilbur J. Cohen, "What Every Social Worker Should Know About Political Action," *Social Work*. Vol. II, No. 3, July 1966, pp. 3-11; and John C. Kidneigh, "Administration and Community Organization in Social Work," in *Readings in Social Work Administration*, John C. Kidneigh, ed., University of Minnesota (mimeo), 1970, p.10.

21. Cohen, *op. cit.*, p. 4.

22. See Peter H. Rossi. "Power and Politics: or Road to Social Reform," *Social Service Review*. Vol. XXXV, No. 4, December 1961, pp. 368-369.

23. Cohen, *op. cit.*, p. 4.

24. *Ibid.*, p. 7.

25. Hugh R. Jones, "Social Policy: We, the People, Must Act," *The Social Welfare Forum, 1968*. New York: Columbia University Press, p. 31.

26. See Alan D. Wade, "The Social Worker in the Political Process," *The Social Welfare Forum, 1966*. New York: Columbia University Press, p. 66.

27. Eidenberg and Morey, *op. cit.*, pp. 216-217.

II

The Social Security Act
of 1935 and Its Significance

There has always been in the United States a struggle against those forces which were too exclusively preoccupied with the organization of economic life and the milking of our resources to give much thought to the human costs or to expend much sympathy on the victims of their work. It has been the function of the liberal tradition in American politics, from the time of Jeffersonian and Jacksonian democracy down through Populism, Progressivism, and the New Deal, at first to broaden the numbers of those who could benefit from the great American bonanza and then to humanize its workings and help heal its casualties. Without this sustained tradition of opposition and protest and reform, the American system would have been, as in times and places it was, nothing but a jungle, and would probably have failed to develop into the remarkable system for production and distribution that it is.

Richard Hoftstadter, *The Age of Reform*. (Alfred A. Knopf, Inc., © 1955.)

THE SIGNIFICANCE OF THE SOCIAL SECURITY ACT is more evident when viewed in the context of the prevailing thought and socio-economic scene prior to 1935, the pressure exerted by reform movements for security, and the leadership exercised by President Roosevelt and his advisers.

It has been said that if Franklin D. Roosevelt had not been the President and if the country had not experienced the Great Depression of the 1930's, no action might have been taken at that time or that the course followed might have been quite different. [1] Undoubtedly President Roosevelt's role was crucial and the Great Depression had a significant impact. What is clear, however, is that no single event, individual, or philosophy determined exclusively the policies and programs embodied in the Social Security Act.

Prevailing Thought and Public Philosophy

The prevailing thought and public philosophy prior to 1935 influenced the way the nation responded to the challenge of poverty and insecurity following the Great Depression. The American poor laws had reflected the opposing philosophies of Social Darwinism and Humanitarianism. The concept of "survival of the fittest" in Social Darwinism, as applied to the life of the individual in society, implied that the competitive process ensured continued improvement. Any attempt to intervene in this natural process was considered unwise; "all attempts to reform social processes," were viewed as "efforts to remedy the irremediable." In this sense Social Darwinistic philosophy discredited efforts at social reform and was, for over a generation, "one of the leading strains in American conservative thought." [2] At the end of the First World War, certainly by 1920, Social Darwinism as a conscious philosophy had disappeared from

the American scene. But Darwinian individualism lingered as a part of "political folklore," even after 1920. [3]

Intertwined with the discredited, but still lingering philosophy of Social Darwinism, was the philosophy of Humanitarianism. It has its roots in the Judeo-Christian tradition of love, brotherhood and charity, which in a sense has been the basis of philanthropy and charitable efforts from the beginning of "the post-Roman western civilization." [4] Humanitarianism with its doctrine that man's obligations are concerned wholly with the welfare of the human race, deriving its strength from the tradition of love, brotherhood and charity, was to conflict with Darwinian individualism.

These opposing philosophies were bound to influence the debate on the issue of the rights of the individual and the extent of authority and obligation of the State, that were brought into the open by concrete proposals for Social Security legislation. It is important to recognize, however, that individualism was the more influential outlook prior to the Great Depression of the 1930's. It was a positive philosophy: personal prosperity was considered a matter of personal initiative and responsibility, and it was incumbent upon each individual to work, save and (therefore) prosper. "The inventiveness of America, its vitality, and its strength, lay in the self-reliance of Americans." [5] The concept of individualism was so much a part of the prevailing social thought that any effort at social reform was viewed as a threat to individual liberty. Proposals for Social Security were viewed not so much in terms of the needs they met, as in terms of the threat to individual freedom that extension of state power posed. [6]

The issue of the role of government and the extent of authority that is to be wielded over the lives of individuals has been a recurrent theme in the history of political philosophy. Throughout American history at every stage when a major new program has been considered, questions have been raised concerning state intervention versus individual freedom. There have also been striking similarities in the arguments raised by opponents to progressive implementation of

welfare state measures. [7] In a sense this is a basic issue that has no closure and is never answered once and for all.

When Social Security proposals urged the necessity of State and Federal action to deal with the problems of old age, destitution, unemployment and sickness, many voices of protest were heard. This went counter to the philosophy of individualism, thrift and self-reliance; nor was there confidence in State and Federal action. In regard to the problems of the aged, there was also the view that it is the duty of the children, rather than that of the State, to assume their care. If the State relieved the children of this responsibility, there was the danger of family ties being loosened; and this threat to the family, the basic social institution, it was felt, could not be risked. [8]

The ideology of Voluntarism which, as Roy Lubove points out, had been a progressive influence in the nineteenth century became regressive in the early part of the twentieth century and stood in the way of governmental efforts to introduce Social Security measures:

> ... by the twentieth century the ideology of voluntarism and the vast network of institutional interests which it had nurtured had become retrogressive in many respects. Assumptions about the self-sufficiency and superiority of voluntary institutions obstructed adaptation to changing economic and social conditions. And nowhere did the rigidities of the voluntary creed prove more disastrous than in the area of social welfare legislation ... voluntarism became, as I. M. Rubinow put it, the great American substitute for social action and policy. What occurred was the creation of socio-economic no-man's-lands; voluntary institutions failed to respond to mass needs, but thwarted governmental efforts to do so. [9]

Voluntarism, implying "action by non-statutory institutions," Lubove maintains, was closely related in American thought to a "cluster of principles"—notably limited government, individual freedom, self-support and an economic system with rewards based on merit in a competitive framework. [10] In the ensuing clash be-

tween the aims of the social insurance movement and the ideology of Voluntarism, the Social Security Act and its provisions emerged as a compromise and a solution at a given time in a particular context.

Socio-Economic Scene, 1930-1935

An examination of the socio-economic scene prior to 1935 and an assessment of the impact of the Great Depression of the 1930's help us to view in perspective the Social Security Act and the policies and programs it ushered in.

The economic system was based on private enterprise and the free market, and the doctrine of individualism exercised strong influence. In socio-economic matters the good of all citizens was held to be realized, by and large, if each person were free to pursue his self-interest with the minimum of government interference. [11] If this approach seemed to have worked hitherto, it was yet to face the challenge of widespread economic and social distress posed by the Great Depression.

A brief look at some key statistical indices, such as population, health, education, unemployment and poverty, will help to understand better the socio-economic scene prior to 1935. One serious limitation in this effort is the lack of complete statistics. At times statistics for the whole country in regard to a particular social problem have been constructed from meager samplings. However, there is reasonably reliable data available to understand the state of affairs between 1930-1935.

In looking at the population trends prior to 1935, it is evident from U.S. Census reports that the birthrate per 1,000 estimated population in the expanding birth-registration area declined from 25.1 in 1915 to 17.1 in 1934—an average of about 2 percent per year.

As a result of this declining birthrate from 1820 onwards the ratio of aged persons (65 years and over) to the total population showed a continuous increase. In 1930 there were about 6½ million

aged persons out of a total population of approximately 122¾ million persons in the United States, representing 5.4 percent of the population. [12] Table 1 indicates the steady rise in the percentage of persons 65 and over in the U.S. from 3.9 to 5.4 percent of the total population, between 1860 and 1930.

The decline in birthrate was not the only cause for the increase in the ratio of aged persons in the population. Life expectancy at birth which also showed an increase was partly responsible. Life expectancy at birth in 1900 was 47.88 for males and 50.70 for females. By the year 1929 the expectancy rates had increased to 57.71 for males and 60.99 for females. [13] Table 2 gives further particulars of the population, with a breakdown by sex and age for 1925-1935.

It should be noted that, along with the increase in the proportion and number of aged persons in the population, there was also an increase in the percentage of gainfully occupied persons, 45 years

TABLE 1

NUMBER OF PERSONS AGED 65 AND OVER COMPARED TO TOTAL POPULATION 1890-1930

Year	Number aged 65 and over	Total population	Percent aged 65 and over
1890	2,424,000	62,622,000	3.9
1900	3,089,000	75,995,000	4.1
1910	3,958,000	91,972,000	4.3
1920	4,940,000	105,711,000	4.7
1930	6,634,000	122,775,000	5.4

Source: *Social Security in America*, Table 26 (adapted). See note 12.

TABLE 2

ESTIMATED POPULATION BY SEX AND AGE
1925 to 1935 (in thousands)

Year	Total	Sex		Age (in Years)						
		Male	Female	Under 14	14 to 24	25 to 34	35 to 44	45 to 54	55 to 64	65 & over
1925	115,832	58,820	57,012	33,677	22,939	18,724	15,578	11,523	7,604	5,788
1926	117,399	59,590	57,809	33,822	23,315	18,866	15,845	11,786	7,804	5,961
1927	119,038	60,402	58,636	33,960	23,733	18,949	16,173	12,093	7,999	6,131
1928	120,501	61,100	59,401	33,966	24,138	18,952	16,538	12,431	8,176	6,298
1929	121,770	61,684	60,086	33,863	24,498	18,942	16,917	12,761	8,315	6,475
1930	123,077	62,297	60,780	33,638	24,852	19,039	17,270	13,096	8,477	6,706
1931	124,040	62,726	61,314	33,442	24,984	19,242	17,412	13,296	8,735	6,929
1932	124,840	63,070	61,770	33,141	25,092	19,484	17,504	13,481	8,992	7,146
1933	125,579	63,384	62,195	32,742	25,221	19,750	17,569	13,684	9,249	7,362
1934	126,374	63,726	62,648	32,294	25,401	20,022	17,640	13,933	9,502	7,583
1935	127,250	64,110	63,140	31,900	25,612	20,275	17,712	14,208	9,739	7,803

Source: U.S. Bureau of the Census, *Historical Statistics of the United States, Colonial Times to 1957*, Washington D.C., 1960, p. 8. Adapted from Series A 22-33.

and over. This situation in which a larger number of older persons were seeking work implied that unless the number of employment opportunities increased at the same rate, this competitive situation was going to impose greater hardship on the older persons. [14] Table 3 indicates that, while in 1890 only 244 out of every 1,000 gainfully occupied persons in the population were 45 or over, by 1930 there were 300 out of every 1,000 in this age group. These demographic facts, which revealed the hardships that the aged were likely to experience coupled with the powerful lobbying of the aged and their spokesmen, helped eventually to make the problem of the aged in the population a central issue in the whole social insurance movement prior to 1935.

In examining the health conditions prior to 1935, one important indicator is the prevailing maternal and infant mortality rates. The U.S. Census reports for 1934 indicate that 12,859 women died from

TABLE 3

PERCENTAGE OF PERSONS 45 YEARS OF AGE AND OVER AMONG GAINFULLY OCCUPIED, BY SEX, FOR THE U.S. 1890-1930

| Year | All Gainfully Occupied | 45 Years and Over | | |
		Total	Male	Female
1890	100.0	24.4	26.4	15.1
1900	100.0	24.1	26.0	15.7
1910	100.0	24.0	26.1	16.0
1920	100.0	27.9	30.4	18.1
1930	100.0	30.0	32.7	20.3

Source: *Social Security in America*, Table 29 (adapted). See note 12.

causes related to pregnancy and childbirth; 130,185 infants died within the first year of life; 43,175 children died between ages 1 and 4 years, inclusive; 37,103 died at ages between 5 and 14 years, inclusive; and 26,885 died between ages 15 and 19 years, inclusive. A further insight into the situation is obtained in examining the extent of stillbirths. Despite the incompleteness in the registration of stillbirths there were 78,503 stillbirths recorded in 1934. It is maintained that the causes of stillbirths and of a fair number of deaths of infants within the first month of life were related to prenatal and natal conditions. [15]

When the maternal mortality rate in the U.S. prior to 1935 is compared with rates available for certain other countries, the U.S. rate is relatively higher. Table 4 indicates the trend in maternal mortality in the U.S., as compared with certain other foreign countries, from 1925 to 1934.

Some questions have been raised about the comparability of maternal mortality rates in the U.S. with other countries prior to 1935, based on the argument that the procedures in ascribing deaths of women to causes related to childbirth vary among countries. [16] But it is maintained that a study made by the Children's Bureau together with the Bureau of Census in 1935 indicates that, though there might be some changes if statistical procedures used in certain foreign countries were utilized, the resulting changes would not be significant, and that the U.S. rates would still be higher than most countries for which data were available. [17]

The reduction in infant mortality rates in the U.S. since the 1920's, when compared with maternal mortality rates, has been significant. There has also been a great variation between states in regard to infant mortality rates. Table 5 illustrates the infant mortality trend for certain states in the U.S. from 1925 to 1934.

The supply of physicians is another possible indicator of the health situation in the country prior to 1935; while the supply had increased since 1900 in numbers it had, however, decreased in proportion to the population. In 1900 there were 173 physicians per 100,000 population; in 1931 there were 126. The total number of

TABLE 4

TREND OF MATERNAL MORTALITY IN THE U.S. AND CERTAIN FOREIGN COUNTRIES—1925-1934

Country	Deaths Assigned to Pregnancy and Childbirth per 10,000 Live Births									
	1925	1926	1927	1928	1929	1930	1931	1932	1933	1934
Canada	56	57	56	56	57	58	51	50	50	53[a]
Denmark	24	27	41	27	32	38	40	35	36	39
England & Wales	41	41	41	44	43	44	41	42	45	46
Irish Free State	47	49	45	49	41	48	43	46	44	44
Italy	28	26	26	28	29	27	28	30	29	27[a]
Lithuania	59	56	50	50	57	60	62	55	61	67
New Zealand	47	42	49	49	48	51	48	41	44	49
Northern Ireland	44	56	48	52	49	53	51	53	54	63
Scotland	62	64	64	70	69	69	59	63	59	63
Uruguay	25	30	22	24	24	31	24	25	24	23
United States:										
Birth-registration area[b]	65	66	65	69	70	67	66	63	62	59
Area of 1921[c]	64	65	62	64	64	62	62	59	58	55

[a] Provisional.

[b] The United States birth-registration area when established in 1915 included 10 States and the District of Columbia; additional States were added as they fulfilled requirements until in 1933 it comprised the entire continental United States.

[c] Birth-registration area of 1921, exclusive of South Carolina, included 26 States and District of Columbia each year.

Source: *Social Security in America*, p. 504. Appendix, Table XI-4 (adapted). See note 12.

TABLE 5

TREND OF INFANT MORTALITY IN THE U.S. BIRTH-REGISTRATION AREA—1925-1934

State	Deaths Under 1 Year per 1,000 Live Births									
	1925	1926	1927	1928	1929	1930	1931	1932	1933	1934
Average, all states	72	73	65	69	68	65	62	58	58	60
Alabama	–	–	64	75	74	72	61	61	65	68
Arkansas	–	–	61	67	58	51	49	45	54	54
Colorado	–	–	–	89	91	94	81	71	69	73
Delaware	91	93	71	78	81	78	82	67	60	61
Georgia	–	–	–	81	76	77	68	64	67	79
Illinois	73	69	64	64	61	56	59	53	49	53
Iowa	56	59	55	53	53	54	49	48	451	
Kentucky	71	75	61	70	71	65	65	63	58	65
Maine	76	80	80	73	77	76	72	63	66	71
Massachusetts	73	73	65	64	62	60	55	53	52	49
Minnesota	60	58	52	54	51	52	51	47	48	47
Missouri	–	–	60	66	62	59	63	57	55	63
Nebraska	58	59	51	53	52	49	49	43	49	45
New Hampshire	76	79	69	69	68	61	57	59	56	61
New Mexico	–	–	–	–	145	145	134	119	136	120
North Carolina	79	82	79	86	79	79	73	67	66	79

Source: U.S. Department of Commerce, Bureau of the Census; *Social Security in America*, p. 505. Appendix, Table XI-5 (adapted). See note 12.

physicians in active practice in the U.S. in 1931 is estimated as approximately 143,299. There was also considerable variation among states in the supply of physicians. There were, in 1931 for example, 178 physicians per 100,000 in California, while in South Carolina there were 74. [18]

Table 6, providing information about specified reportable diseases between 1929 and 1935, gives further insights into the health conditions prior to 1935.

A fair assessment of the educational situation prior to 1935 could be made from available statistical data pertaining to elementary and secondary schools in the U.S. The prevailing educational system was

TABLE 6

SPECIFIED REPORTABLE DISEASES—1929-1935
(Rate per 100,000 Population Estimated as of July 1, for Each Year)

Year	Typhoid & Para-typhoid Fever	Scarlet Fever & Strepto-coccal Throat	Dipth-eria	Whoop-ing Cough	Menningo-coccal Infections	Acute Polio-myelitis	Small-pox
1929	19.1	152.9	70.1	162.1	8.7	2.4	34.7
1930	22.1	144.5	54.1	135.6	7.0	7.7	39.7
1931	21.4	166.3	57.1	139.1	4.7	13.3	24.4
1932	21.4	172.7	48.0	172.5	2.6	3.1	9.0
1933	18.6	174.4	40.2	142.6	2.4	4.0	5.2
1934	17.6	180.0	34.1	209.9	2.0	5.9	4.3
1935	14.4	211.1	30.8	141.9	4.7	8.5	6.3

Source: U.S. Bureau of the Census, *Historical Statistics of the United States, Colonial Times to 1957*, Washington, D.C., 1960, p. 38. Adapted from Series B 275-281.

unique in comparison with European countries in that it had long provided a single line of progress from the primary school to the university. Whatever educational opportunities available were open to all classes of children. Schools were largely controlled by local authorities and the federal government exercised no direct control.

The development of American schools from 1900 to 1930 indicates that education had become a "major public interest." In 1900 there were 284,683 students in universities, colleges and teacher training institutions in the U.S. By 1930, while the U.S. population increased only 62 percent, the attendance in institutions of higher education had increased by 314 percent, with 1,178,318 students. The number of students in secondary schools had also increased from 630,048 in 1900 to 4,740,580 in 1930. In 1930 one of every seven persons of college age was in college and one of every two persons of secondary school age was in high school. [19] Table 7 gives particulars regarding enrollment and attendance in elementary and secondary schools and the number of high school graduates in the U.S. from 1924 to 1934.

In regard to employment and poverty prior to 1935 the data available are relatively limited and less reliable. Nevertheless it is possible to make a fair estimation of the prevailing conditions. Unemployment in the 1930's was becoming widespread and was the key to a substantial amount of the prevailing dependency and poverty. The situation was complicated even more by the varying incidence of unemployment as between states and industries. While the 1930-1933 unemployment average was 25.8 percent for the whole country it was 34.3 percent in Michigan, for example. Comparatively, unemployment was more severe in manufacturing and mining than in the service industries. [20]

The following table indicates the unemployment situation in the U.S. from 1929-1935. The table indicates that the peak year of unemployment during this period was 1933, when the total unemployed amounted to nearly 13 million. Economic historians vary in their estimate of the number unemployed during the peak year;

TABLE 7

ELEMENTARY AND SECONDARY SCHOOLS: ENROLLMENT AND ATTENDANCE AND HIGH SCHOOL GRADUATES—1924 to 1934

School Year Ending	School Enrollment						Public School Average Daily Attendance (All Grades)	High School Graduates [c]
	Public Day Schools					*Non-public Schools* [b]		
	Totals: [a] Public Day Schools and Non-public Schools	Totals: Public Day Schools	Totals as Percent of Population 5 to 17 Years Old	Kindergarten and Grades 1 to 8	Grades 9 to 12 and Post-graduates			
1924	26,016,072	24,288,808	82.8	20,898,930	3,389,878	1,727,264	19,132,451	494,006
1926	27,180,193	24,741,468	82.3	20,984,002	3,757,466	2,438,725	19,855,881	561,469
1928	27,810,309	25,179,696	81.5	21,268,417	3,911,279	2,630,613	20,608,353	596,655
1930	28,329,059	25,678,015	81.3	21,278,593	4,399,422	2,651,044	21,264,886	666,904
1932	29,061,403	26,275,441	82.0	21,135,420	5,140,021	2,785,962	22,245,344	826,991
1934	29,162,732	26,434,193	81.6	20,765,037	5,669,156	2,728,539	22,458,190	914,853

[a] Partially estimated. Includes enrollment in regular public and non-public day schools. Excludes pupils enrolled in residential schools for exceptional children, subcollegiate departments of institutions of higher education, and Federal schools.

[b] Partially estimated.

[c] Includes graduates from public and nonpublic schools. Nonpublic graduates are partially estimated.

Source: U.S. Bureau of the Census, *Historical Statistics of the United States, Colonial Times to 1957*, Washington, D.C., 1960, p. 207. Adapted from Series H 223-233.

some estimate the number unemployed to be as high as 16 million (see Table 8).

In addition to data on unemployment, statistics regarding cost of living also helps considerably in the attempt to understand the socio-economic scene. Table 9 indicates the cost of living in the U.S. for the period from June 1929 to December 1933.

The index of wages per hour, like the cost of living index is also helpful in giving insights into the socio-economic situation. But perhaps what is most helpful is the index of the worker's "real wage." Table 10 provides the index numbers of wages per hour, cost of living and "real wages" for the years 1925 to 1932.

It has been estimated that during the time of the depression, one-fourth of the nation's workers were unemployed and about one-fifth of the nation subsisted on directed relief or work relief. [21] In the face of mounting unemployment the prevailing

TABLE 8

UNEMPLOYMENT: 1929-1935
(Annual averages of persons 14 years
old and over.)

Year	Unemployed	Percent of Civilian Labor Force
1929	1,550,000	3.2
1930	4,340,000	8.7
1931	8,020,000	15.9
1932	12,060,000	23.6
1933	12,830,000	24.9
1934	11,340,000	21.7
1935	10,610,000	20.1

Source: U.S. Bureau of the Census, *Historical Statistics of the United States, Colonial Times to 1957*, Washington, D.C., 1960, p. 73. Adapted from Series D 46-47.

TABLE 9

COST OF LIVING IN THE UNITED STATES
INDEX NUMBERS, JUNE 1929-DECEMBER 1933

Note: 1913 average = 100. Figures for food represent 51 cities since 1920; other figures represent 32 cities. Totals weighted by relative importance of items as ascertained by country-wide study of cost of living.

Date		All Items	Food	Clothing	Hous-ing	Fuel, Light	Furniture, Furnishings	Misc.
June	1929	170.2	154.8	161.3	153.7	175.2	198.5	207.3
Dec.	1929	171.4	158.0	160.5	151.9	178.7	197.7	207.9
June	1930	166.6	147.9	158.9	149.6	172.8	195.7	208.5
Dec.	1930	160.7	137.2	153.0	146.5	175.0	188.3	208.1
June	1931	150.3	118.3	146.0	142.0	165.4	177.0	206.6
Dec.	1931	145.8	114.3	135.5	136.2	168.0	167.1	205.4
June	1932	135.7	100.1	127.8	127.8	157.1	153.4	202.1
Dec.	1932	132.1	98.7	121.5	118.0	156.9	147.4	199.3
June	1933	128.3	96.7	119.8	108.8	148.4	147.7	194.5
Dec.	1933	135.0	105.5	133.6	104.1	159.3	164.8	195.9

Source: Bureau of Labor Statistics, Department of Labor; U.S. Bureau of Foreign and Domestic Commerce, *Statistical Abstract of the United States, 1934*, Washington, D.C., 1934, pp. 289-290. Adapted from No. 320.

system of public relief, which was by and large "improvised in the course of depression," was also breaking down. In mid-1934 approximately one out of every seven persons in the country, more than 18 million people, were on relief. Almost 7 million children under 16 years of age were on the rolls. Unemployment and poverty were spread across the country. In 39 states over one-tenth of the population was dependent on public funds. In some states the proportion was more: South Dakota, which was afflicted by the

TABLE 10

INDEX NUMBERS OF WAGES PER HOUR,
COST OF LIVING,

Note: The general trend of wages per hour relates to the money received per hour by the wage earner as compensation for his work. The real measure of his wage, however, is not his money income, but what he is able to buy with it. In the following table, therefore, index numbers relating to wages per hour and to cost of living are brought together, and from them a third index number is computed showing the change in the worker's "real wage."

Year	Index Numbers (1910 = 100)		
	Wages per Hour	*Cost of Living*	*Real Wages*
1925	226	175.7	128.6
1926	229	175.2	130.7
1927	231	172.7	133.8
1928	232	170.7	135.9
1929	233	170.8	136.4
1930	229	163.7	139.9
1931	217	148.1	146.5
1932	186	133.9	138.9

Source: Bureau of Labor Statistics, Department of Labor; *Statistical Abstract of this United States, 1934, ibid.*, p. 296. Adapted from No. 328.

drought, had over one-third of the population dependent on public funds. [22]

The Federal Emergency Relief Administration's Unemployment Relief Census of October 1933 indicates the number of families receiving public unemployment relief by states, as seen in Table 11.

It is evident that the heavily industrial states of Pennsylvania, New York, Illinois, Ohio, and Michigan had a relatively large number of families receiving public unemployment relief.

TABLE 11

TOTAL NUMBER OF FAMILIES RECEIVING PUBLIC UNEMPLOYMENT RELIEF, OCTOBER 1933 BY STATES AND DISTRICT OF COLUMBIA

Rank	State	Number of Families	Rank	State	Number of Families
1.	Pennsylvania	324,461	25.	Minnesota	45,358
2.	New York	311,983	26.	Tennessee	39,312
3.	Illinois	234,727	27.	Washington	37,877
4.	Ohio	202,865	28.	Iowa	35,051
5.	Michigan	152,679	29.	Maryland	31,817
6.	California	118,264	30.	Connecticut	23,961
7.	Oklahoma	107,237	31.	Colorado	22,815
8.	Texas	105,045	32.	South Dakota	22,382
9.	Florida	102,432	33.	Arizona	20,427
10.	Kentucky	98,883	34.	Montana	18,882
11.	Alabama	98,648	35.	Oregon	16,666
12.	Massachusetts	89,848	36.	Utah	16,354
13.	South Carolina	89,326	37.	Virginia	14,983
14.	West Virginia	86,342	38.	Nebraska	13,844
15.	New Jersey	84,452	39.	Dist. of Col.	12,228
16.	Lousiana	76,751	40.	Rhode Island	10,684
17.	Indiana	76,649	41.	North Dakota	10,020
18.	Georgia	69,588	42.	Maine	8,884
19.	Wisconsin	67,352	43.	New Mexico	6,587
20.	Missouri	57,165	44.	Delaware	5,862
21.	North Carolina	56,041	45.	Idaho	5,433
22.	Mississippi	54,559	46.	New Hampshire	5,030
23.	Arkansas	48,331	47.	Nevada	2,946
24.	Kansas	46,221	48.	Vermont	2,817
			49.	Wyoming	1,482

Source: U.S. Federal Emergency Relief Administration, *Unemployment Relief Census, 1933*, Washington, D.C., 1934, p. 4. Adapted from Chart 1.

The significant facts regarding the unemployment relief situation revealed by the Unemployment Relief Census of October 1933 were: the regional concentration of relief persons, the noticeable differences in the proportion of white, Negro and other races on relief, the increasing number of large families among the relief cases and the disproportionately large number of children as compared with the general population. The regional concentration was evident in that in three states approximately a quarter of the total population was on relief while the average for the whole country was about 10 percent. Negroes on relief were approximately twice as great in proportion to their numbers in the population as were whites. Small families (2 to 4 persons) were less frequently on relief than large families (5 or more persons). However, one-person families were an appreciable proportion—13 percent of all relief families and over 3 percent of all relief recipients. [23] Table 12, indicating the total number of persons receiving emergency relief and the obligations incurred for emergency relief from public funds between 1933 and 1935 in the U.S., further illuminates the relief situation prior to 1935.

Impact of the Great Depression

The Great Depression of the 1930's, the worst economic crisis in the nation's history, necessitated significant changes in philosophy, policy and programs in the social welfare field. The crash of the stock market and the dislocation of the economic system undermined faith in individualism and business practices. The economic crisis eventually turned out to be "a political and ideological crisis as well." [24]

President Hoover, who reflected the views of the conservative forces in the country, denied at the outset the need for any change or governmental intervention. In the 1928 presidential campaign, Herbert Hoover had acclaimed the solution of socio-economic problems automatically by the business process as "our American experiment in human welfare." [25]

TABLE 12

UNEMPLOYMENT RELIEF: PERSONS RECEIVING EMERGENCY RELIEF AND OBLIGATIONS INCURRED FOR EMERGENCY RELIEF FROM ALL PUBLIC FUNDS, 1933 to 1935

Year and Month	Total Number of Persons Receiving Relief (thousands) [a]	Obligations Incurred for Relief (thousands of dollars) [b]				Source of Funds		Average Amount of Relief Extended per Family per Month [d]
		Total	Direct Relief	Work Relief [c]	All Other	Federal	State, Local	
1933		$792,788	[f]	[f]	[f]	$480,673	$312,115	[f]
January [e]	17,300 [e]	60,827	[f]	[f]	[f]	31,175	29,652	[f]
June [e]	16,900 [e]	66,338	$39,425	$22,630	$4,283	42,464	23,874	$15.95
1934		1,475,792	656,537	457,412	361,843	1,063,413	412,379	
January [g]	11,084	54,109	43,753	1,560	8,796	29,271	24,838	17.15
June	16,829	125,401	51,104	42,424	31,873	91,497	33,904	23.84
1935		1,827,994	1,834,411	515,813	477,770	1,359,921	468,073	
Jan.	20,686	196,511	77,535	70,902	48,074	151,886	44,625	30.45
June	17,961	169,471	62,681	54,384	52,406	130,102	39,369	28.17

[a] Covers the general relief program (direct relief and work relief) and special programs (rural rehabilitation, emergency education, and college student aid).

[b] Includes, in addition to direct relief and work relief, obligations incurred for relief under the special programs, for administration, and, since April 1934, for purchases of materials, supplies, and equipment, rental of equipment, earnings of non-relief persons employed, and other expenses incident to the Emergency Work Relief Program, which in this Table are combined in the column headed "All Other."

[c] Beginning with April 1934, represents earnings of relief persons under the Emergency Work Relief Program.

[d] Covers only direct relief and Emergency Work Relief Program earnings of families under the general relief program.

[e] Estimated. [f] Data are not available. [g] Figures do not include activities conducted under the Civil Works Program.

Source: Federal Emergency Relief Administration; Bureau of Foreign and Domestic Commerce, *Statistical Abstract of the United States, 1936*, *Washington, D.C., 1936, p. 334. Adapted from No. 373.*

The Great Depression, the resultant economic collapse and the unprecedented social misery were to reveal the hollowness of Hoover's utterances. It is a popular but mistaken notion that the depression disrupted an otherwise secure socio-economic system in a sort of "spontaneous combustion." [26] In fact many concerned leaders and organizations for several years before the depression had urged the need to tackle the problem of inadequate provisions against poverty and dependency. The President's Research Committee on Social Trends, appointed in the autumn of 1929 by Hoover, stated emphatically in its report that

... the major emerging problem is that of closer coordination and more effective integration of the swiftly changing elements in American social life. [27]

It went on to point out that the first prerequisite in tackling this problem was the

... willingness and determination to undertake important social changes in the reorganization of social life, including the economic and political orders, rather than the pursuance of a policy of drift. [28]

The Committee, fully conscious of its mission and the importance of speaking out in the situation of possible dangers in a policy of prolonged social drift, stated that it did not

... wish to assume an attitude of alarmist irresponsibility, but on the other hand it would be highly negligent to gloss over the stark and bitter realities of the social situation, and to ignore the imminent perils in further advance of our heavy technical machinery over crumbling roads and shaking bridges. There are times when silence is not neutrality, but assent. [29]

Such warning of the need for a constructive social policy and initiative was not taken seriously.

The several millions facing unemployment following the Great Depression offered the best example of poverty which was not the result of individual failure or unwillingness to work. It brought into the open for questioning, the "comfortable economic assumptions of the American people." Individuals who had shared with President Hoover the philosophy that "hard work and ability" and the "spirit of charity and mutual self-help" were adequate to meet the needs of all persons in each community, witnessed the situation of whole communities being improverished. [30] Social workers, such as Lillian Wald of the Henry Street Settlement and Clarence Pickett of the Friends Service Committee, pressed for Federal assistance. President Hoover, however, continued to argue that voluntary agencies could meet the problem of the unemployed. [31] It was several months after the stock market crash of 1929 when President Hoover conceded the seriousness of the economic situation and the need for remedial measures. Bremner's comments on the nature of the remedial measures undertaken indicate how hopelessly inadequate Hoover's efforts to meet the situation were:

> The Hoover Administration then undertook such measures to promote recovery as were consistent with the President's philosophy of government. Even, so the Administration retained the outlook of the 1920's and, as Franklin D. Roosevelt observed, the program it adopted to meet the emergency delayed relief and neglected reform. [32]

As the crisis following the depression deepened it undoubtedly shook the American people out of lethargy in facing up to problems of mass poverty and dependency. It bore witness to the folly of attempts to hold back reform efforts and needed institutional changes. The American people were shocked into a realization of the need for government action to meet the situation. The voluntary agencies could hardly cope with the situation of large-scale unemployment and dependency. It was inevitable that the Federal government enter the scene to combat the problems and distress of such magnitude.

While it is true that the Great Depression had a significant impact on the nation and that there is perhaps considerable justification for the view that "the Social Security Act was a child of the Great Depression," it is debatable whether the depression was solely responsible for ushering in the reform measures of the New Deal and for the government's efforts to deal with socio-economic problems from a long-term perspective. [33] There were other actors in the scene—the social reformers, the reform movements, President Roosevelt and his advisers—all of whom contributed to the emergence of a new outlook and the development of a more constructive policy to meet the problems of poverty and insecurity.

Role of Reformers and Movements

The pressure for Social Security measures before 1930, specifically by organized groups, was not so strong or sustained when compared with efforts in other western countries. There has been in the United States a "historical lag" in the introduction of these measures perhaps explainable in part by the fact that frontier resources, particularly land available at nominal or no charge, tended to be an open door and a form of Social Security in the nineteenth century. [34]

Prior to the establishment of the American Association for Labor Legislation (AALL) in 1906, social insurance had not been seriously debated in the United States. [35] AALL to a large extent initiated and developed the social insurance movement. It was an "informal coalition" of reform-minded leaders, representing a variety of interest groups, such as doctors, lawyers, businessmen, labor leaders, politicians, social workers and educators, and exercised considerable influence in the early years, largely as a result of the very nature of its membership. [36] Under the leadership of its Executive Secretary, John B. Andrews, AALL focused attention on the issue of social insurance, along with accident compensation, industrial safety, and unemployment. [37] To begin with, the experience of AALL in the area of workmen's compensation was encouraging. But the

health insurance campaign of 1915-1920 under AALL resulted in failure. Despite this, the social insurance movement continued through the 1920's and "persisted as an issue in American social politics." Along with the earlier leadership of AALL, Andrews and Rubinow, there emerged new social reformers, notably Abraham Epstein, Eveline Burns and Paul Douglas, to carry the social insurance movement forward. [38]

There were by and large two "main streams of thinking" and "resultant political pressures" by the 1930's—"the social insurance concept" and the "idea of flat pensions"—spearheaded by two different movements. [39] The social insurance concept as noted earlier had by this time several concerned spokesmen, such as Andrews, Rubinow, Epstein, Douglas, Commons and Burns, though not all had similar views. [40] In a sense it was Abraham Epstein who became the chief spokesman for the concept of social insurance. He worked untiringly to advance its cause through his organization, the American Association for Old-Age Security, founded in 1927, which in 1933 broadened its objectives and adopted the name of American Association for Social Security. The Townsend Movement, started in California by Dr. Frank E. Townsend in 1933, championed the cause of the flat pension idea. A flat pension of $200 per month financed by a sales tax was to be made available to all persons aged sixty years and over. The Townsend Movement grew rapidly, and within two years there were 4,550 Townsend clubs all over the country. [41]

The old-age revolving pension plan of Dr. Townsend, an "economic amateur," was scoffed at by the economists of the day. They argued that, even if the rest of the plan were feasible, the sales tax necessary to finance it would be so great that trade would be seriously hampered. [42] But this did not prevent the Townsend Movement from exercising considerable political influence in the country and exerting pressure to make adequate provisions for old age security. In certain electorates the Townsend pension plan emerged as the key issue and congressional candidates were elected on the basis of their support for the program. The Townsend Movement posed the threat of more fundamental change and in this

way exercised strong pressure for action. It was a fair indicator of the public's feelings, particularly those of the aged, toward old age security.

President Roosevelt is reported to have told his Secretary of Labor, Frances Perkins, that the Committee on Economic Security headed by her had to come up with some concrete plans for a system of social insurance, since

> ... the Congress can't stand the pressure of the Townsend Plan unless we have a real old-age insurance system, nor can I face the people without having ... a solid plan which will give some assurance to people of systematic assistance upon retirement. [43]

Undoubtedly, the President himself was an advocate of social insurance and was committed to meeting the challenge of insecurity and required no "prodding," but the threat of extreme movements such as the Townsend Movement and Senator Huey Long's Share the Wealth Movement, undoubtedly helped in obtaining congressional approval for the passage of the Social Security Act. [44]

The pressure exerted by these extreme movements and the panaceas offered should not blind us to the role of several other voluntary movements that did not have such a dramatic impact, but nevertheless made their contribution to the ongoing cause of reform and the "struggle" for social security. Reference has already been made to the role of the American Association for Labor Legislation and the American Association for Old Age Security which later became the American Association for Social Security. In addition to these, there were such voluntary organizations as the National Consumers League, the American Association of Social Workers [45], the National Conference of Social Work (later to become the National Conference on Social Welfare), the League of Women Voters and the National Federation of Settlements that kept alive the reform spirit. It was the "reform impulse" of these organizations and the reformers associated with them in the 1920's that justify the title of

Clarke Chambers' study, *Seedtime of Reform,* even though "so far as conditions of the poor and the indigent were concerned," Irwin Bernstein's title of the *The Lean Years,* for his study of the labor movement would be more fitting. [46]

The labor movement, which had given considerable support to the cause of social security in Britain and Europe, did very little to advance the social insurance movement in the United States in the early stages. This void was ably filled by the efforts of the social reformers and their voluntary organizations. [47] A good many of these social reformers, such as Jane Addams, Lillian Wald, Graham Taylor, John B. Andrews, Florence Kelley and Paul Kellogg, emerged out of "prewar progressivism." Others like Abraham Epstein, John R. Commons, Isaac Rubinow, Gertrude Vaile and Eduard Lindeman had been influenced by progressivism, but emerged as leaders only after the "inter-war era." There were still others who were relatively newcomers, such as Paul Douglas, Harry Hopkins, Frances Perkins, Mary Dewson, Edwin E. Witte, Arthur J. Altmeyer and Jane Hoey, who were also to play a key role in carrying the reform impulse forward. [48]

These social reformers and their respective organizations in many instances studied the problems of social security, developed their own leadership, kept politicians, community leaders and others concerned informed of the socio-economic problems, and prepared legislative schemes that could be acted on when the time was ripe. [49] Through the medium of the *Survey,* a journal devoted to social reform, Paul Kellogg, its editor, kept alive the interest in social insurance, particularly unemployment insurance. Likewise, the publication in the 1930's of three important works with direct bearing on social security—Abraham Epstein's *Insecurity,* Isaac Rubinow's *Quest for Security* and Paul Douglas's *The Problem of Unemployment*—helped to focus national attention on the problem. [50]

It is clear that, following the Great Depression, the public demand for Social Security under the leadership of reformers and the different movements was mounting. Some plans were dubbed "crack-pot schemes," others were viewed with favor, but they all

exerted pressure in varying degrees. It was left to the leadership of President Roosevelt and his skillful advisers to interpret the mood to Congress and to adopt the necessary strategy for its enactment of the Social Security Act.

Leadership of President Roosevelt and His Advisers

Franklin Delano Roosevelt became President at a time when, following the depression, the socio-economic system was subject to searching questions; it had "halted at dead center." The "New Deal" that he ushered in was named after Theodore Roosevelt's "Square Deal" and Wilson's "New Freedom." [51] There is the tendency in the interest of continuity to see the New Deal as an extension of the concerns of Progressivism and the reform efforts begun under Theodore Roosevelt and Woodrow Wilson. Hofstadter maintains that, while there may be an element of continuity, what seems significant about the New Deal is the dramatic change and break with past American reform efforts. The New Deal was different in regard to its central problem, its ideas, spirit and techniques. [52]

It is important, however, to note that the New Deal lacked a cohesive philosophy. It tried different approaches in the attempt to meet the socio-economic problems of the day and there was no clear line of ideology. It has been suggested that perhaps the only element that was a common link to the different approaches was the role of the federal government "as an energizing force." [53] The following incident perhaps illustrates in a humorous way the lack of a coherent theory or principles in the New Deal:

> . . . In the heat of the presidential campaign of 1936, the local Democratic headquarters received a telephone call. "Say," a voice exclaimed, "tell us just what the principles of the New Deal are—we're having an argument." "Hold the phone," was the answering injunction, followed by a long pause. Then: "Sorry. We're having an argument too." [54]

The New Dealers, under the leadership of Franklin Roosevelt, were concerned more with action than with ideological debates and tended to "play it by ear." Needless to say, Roosevelt had among his advisers highly educated persons—in fact, political cartoons of the day pictured his advisers as wearing academic caps and gowns. But it is evident that the typical New Dealer, whether highly educated or not, was "a social engineer rather than an intellectual." As represented in Harry Hopkins's work and contribution, the emphasis was on experimentation, hopefully successful experimentation. [55] Effective action to combat the massive problems of the day was what Roosevelt had promised under the "New Deal." There were several agencies set up to combat the problems posed by the depression, notably the Federal Emergency Relief Administration, Works Progress Administration, Civil Works Administration, Civilian Conservation Corps and National Recovery Administration.

The President courageously pursued a policy of developing long-range programs to meet the basic problems of insecurity highlighted by the depression, in addition to the task of giving help on an emergency basis. The leadership that he exercised in this regard is significant in the context of the demand in certain quarters that "recovery must precede reform." [56] It is also fortunate that Roosevelt had among his advisers persons such as Frances Perkins, Secretary of Labor, and Harry Hopkins, Federal Emergency Relief Administrator, who shared his enthusiasm and who had the combination of dedication, experience and expertise.

Harry Hopkins reflected the spirit of the New Dealers by his emphasis on effective action to meet the hardship and the misery caused by the depression and by his inclination, as he put it, "to leave philosophizing about relief to others." While excessive philosophizing about relief was considered a luxury, emphasis was laid on study and research before action. "We consider the work of our division of research and statistics," stated Hopkins, "to be of equal importance with the administration of relief." [57] Hopkins also pointed to tasks beyond relief, of the necessity of changes in the economic system itself:

... it is easy to see that effective relief methods—that is practices which will take us out of the necessity for relief—will eventually have to change certain practices of our economic system. ... We know where poverty is, and where it will continue to be, so long as certain practices of our economic system are allowed to persist. [58]

Leadership of this caliber helped considerably in what Roosevelt termed "bold, persistent experimentation," and in the efforts to develop long-term solutions to the problems of poverty and basic insecurity.

The Social Security proposals that the President presented to Congress were designed to meet the criticisms of the immediate relief programs and to aim at long-term solutions. In his presidential message on June 8, 1934, Roosevelt had already promised the country legislation on the subject of Social Security:

> Among our objectives I place the security of the men, women, and children of the Nation first.
> This security for the individual and for the family concerns itself primarily with three factors. People want decent homes to live in; they want to locate them where they can engage in productive work; and they want some safeguard against misfortunes which cannot be wholly eliminated in this man-made world of ours. [59]

He also indicated what he considered to be the basis of a sound Social Security program—a state-federal program financed by contributory insurance rather than by an increase in general taxation.

In pursuance of this intention, the President, by Executive Order No. 6757 of June 29, 1934, established a Cabinet Committee on Economic Security consisting of: Frances Perkins, Secretary of Labor (chairman); Henry Morgenthau, Jr., Secretary of the Treasury; Homer Cummings, Attorney General; Henry A. Wallace, Secretary of Agriculture; and Harry L. Hopkins, Federal Emergency Relief Administrator. [60] The Committee was to study the entire problem of economic security and to report not later than December 1, 1934

with recommendations which were to serve as the basis for Social Security legislation by Congress. There was the instruction to consider "all forms of social insurance." The committee on Economic Security was assisted in its task by a Technical Board consisting of government officials who were considered experts in specific areas, with Arthur J. Altmeyer as chairman; an Advisory Council consisting of persons outside of government, representing labor, employer groups and social welfare; and an executive director in the person of Dr. Edwin E. Witte. The Advisory Council was to convey to the Committee on Economic Security the thinking and opinions of interested groups and individuals outside government in regard to Social Security. Eight additional advisory committees were also created later, pertaining to special aspects of the problems of Social Security. [61]

Among the executive staff of the Committee on Economic Security was Wilbur J. Cohen, research assistant to the executive director, who in the years following the passage of the Social Security Act was to play an increasingly significant role. In the Old Age Security staff of the committee there were persons such as Barbara Armstrong and Douglas J. Brown, and in the Employment Opportunities staff, Eveline Burns and others of her caliber whose skills and experience were available.

These advisers from social welfare and related fields, notably Perkins, Hopkins, Altmeyer and Witte, played an important role in keeping alive the determination to make Social Security a reality, in making available their technical expertise and in helping to develop feasible measures. The Social Security bill that was passed in 1935 by Congress, based largely on the recommendations of the President, and his Economic Security Committee, emerged as a compromise in the face of conflicting interests and pressures.

Basic Provisions of the Social Security Act

It is not the intention here to examine in any great detail the various provisions of the Social Security Act of 1935. Rather, what is

attempted is a brief look at some of the more important provisions of the Act. It is interesting to note that the main features of the programs ushered in by the Social Security Act were largely on the lines advocated by the President's Committee on Economic Security, whose reports and recommendations provided the basis for the Act. Also the Committee, apart from taking into consideration the ideas of the President in regard to Social Security, gave due attention in making its recommendations to questions of constitutionality, "congressional reactions" and similar practical concerns to ensure adoption. [62]

At the very early stages of the Committee on Economic Security's deliberations, it had come to grips with basic policy questions regarding which decisions had to be made in the light of presidential preferences, political pressures, and similar considerations. Among them were such questions as these:

Is the social insurance system to be federally administered, or is it to be state administered, but with standards set by the federal government . . . ?

Should the Committee develop its program on the assumption that it is to be essentially post-recovery in its application or is it to come into effect before there has been complete recovery? [63]

Policy positions varied among the committee members, the experts who were advisers to the Committee, and interest groups in the community. Despite such differences the Committee, after considerable questioning, deliberation and consultation, came up with its recommendations.

The Committee in making its recommendations viewed social insurance as the "first line of defense" against poverty and dependency, and public assistance as "a second line" to be resorted to if the first line proved inadequate. [64] The recommendations made by the Committee included the following:

A federal system of compulsory old-age insurance.

A voluntary government plan of old-age annuities.

A federal-state system of unemployment insurance.

Federal grants to the states to enable them to provide public assistance to dependent children and elderly who were otherwise unprovided for.

Federal grants to the states to enable them to meet the expenses of public health and child welfare services. [65]

It should be noted that not all the recommendations of the Committee on Economic Security were embodied in the Social Security Act. The recommendation for the introduction of a voluntary government plan of old age annuities, for example, was dropped. The Act, however, incorporated the basic recommendations of the Committee. Social reformers and legislators who had hoped for comprehensive social legislation were disappointed in the provisions of the Social Security Act; others reasoned that the Act was "as ambitious as the prevailing cultural milieu would permit." [66]

The basic provisions of the Social Security Act were intended to meet the situation of poverty and dependency, both immediate and long-term. Accordingly, there were two types of public measures introduced—social or public assistance and social insurance. The Act provided for a Federal compulsory old-age insurance program; a state-operated system of unemployment insurance; grants to the states for maternal and child welfare, for aid to dependent children, for aid to the blind, for old-age assistance and for public health work. [67] The Act also set up the Social Security Board—an independent agency to supervise the administration of the social insurance and public assistance programs provided under the Social Security Act.

Provision of insurance for the aged was assured by the Federal Old Age Benefits title of the Social Security Act. According to Title

II of the Act every qualified individual was to be entitled upon reaching age 65 or on January 1, 1942, whichever was later, to an old-age benefit for life. [68] These retirement benefits or annuities were to be financed by direct contributions from employees and employers. It is estimated that about 26,000,000 persons were eligible to contribute in terms of the qualifications specified by the Act. [69] But there were several classifications of workers, nearly half the working population, left uncovered.

The monthly benefits payable to qualified persons after 65 were to be determined by the total amount of wages from employment that was covered by the old-age benefits provisions of the Act. There was the requirement that the individual must have worked at some time for at least five years after 1936 and before the age of 65. It was also necessary that the wages from such employment should amount to at least $2,000. The monthly benefit was to be paid at the rate of one-half of 1 percent of the first $3,000 of the total wages, plus one-twelfth of 1 percent of the next $42,000, plus one-twenty-fourth of 1 percent of any further amount. [70] In utilizing a higher percentage of the first $3,000 of total wages, the benefit scale was intended to give greater weight to the earnings of low-income, middle-aged and older workers than to those of persons who, by virtue of long periods of employment and possibly high salaries, had accumulated larger sums as total wages. [71] Table 13 indicates the varying monthly benefits payable to individuals who qualify under the old-age insurance provisions of the Social Security Act.

It will be noted that the smallest monthly benefit payable was $10 (provided the aggregate of wages from employment was at least $2,000) and that the maximum benefit as specified by the Act was $85 a month. This limit imposed on the maximum benefit payment possible, irrespective of salary or length of service, was also designed to give greater weight to the earnings of low-income and older workers. It is provisions such as these that could perhaps lend support to the claim that the American Social Security system, while involving the highly paid worker, ingeniously provided for indirect

TABLE 13

MONTHLY BENEFITS PAYABLE FOR SPECIFIED TOTAL WAGES AS DEFINED FOR THE PURPOSES OF THE II OF THE SOCIAL SECURITY ACT [a]

Total Wages	Monthly Benefit at Specified Rate				Total Wages	Monthly Benefit at Specified Rate			
	0.5% of first $3,000	1/12 of 1% of next $42,000	1/24 of 1% of all over $45,000	Total		0.5% of first $3,000	1/12 of 1% of next $42,000	1/24 of 1% of all over $45,000	Total
$ 2,000	$10.00	---	---	$10.00	$ 35,000	$15.00	$26.67	---	$41.67
2,500	12.50	---	---	12.50	40,000	15.00	30.83	---	45.83
3,000	15.00	---	---	15.00	45,000	15.00	35.00	---	50.00
3,500	15.00	$ 0.42	---	15.42	50,000	15.00	35.00	$ 2.08	52.08
4,000	15.00	0.83	---	15.83	60,000	15.00	35.00	6.25	56.25
4,500	15.00	1.25	---	16.25	70,000	15.00	35.00	10.42	60.42
5,000	15.00	1.67	---	16.67	80,000	15.00	35.00	14.58	64.58
10,000	15.00	5.83	---	20.83	90,000	15.00	35.00	18.75	68.75
15,000	15.00	10.00	---	25.00	100,000	15.00	35.00	22.92	72.92
20,000	15.00	14.17	---	29.17	110,000	15.00	35.00	27.08	77.08
25,000	15.00	18.33	---	33.33	120,000	15.00	35.00	31.25	81.25
30,000	15.00	22.50	---	37.50	130,000	15.00	35.00	35.42	[b] 85.00

[a] 49 Stat. 622 Sections 201-210; 42 U.S.C. (1935 Supp.) Sections 401-410.
[b] Maximum monthly benefit.
Source: U.S. Committee on Economic Security. Social Security in America, op. cit., p. 224, Table 48.

redistribution of some wealth from the rich to the poor. The European experiment of flat pensions had resulted in the highly paid workers' not being involved in the social insurance program. However there were social reformers, notably Epstein, who were to criticize this very arrangement in the American Social Security system as token redistribution, demanding that much more should be done in this direction.

The unemployment insurance provisions of the Act introduced what is often termed a federal-state system of unemployment compensation. The Social Security Act provided for the levy by the federal government of an excise tax on the payrolls of employers in the commercial and industrial fields. As an inducement for the states to establish programs which conformed to certain standards, it was stipulated that wherever a state unemployment system was introduced, 90 percent of the taxes collected would be credited to the state fund. [72] Essentially the unemployment insurance program was, and even to this day is, a state-administered program.

The failure of the Social Security Act to provide for a national system of unemployment compensation and national standards has been the subject of much criticism. For example, the Social Security Act had among its objectives the discouragement of interstate competition as a hindrance to the adoption of state unemployment insurance laws, but the Act itself introduced interstate competition by permitting individual states to decide on the effective rates of taxation. [73] Arthur Schlesinger, commenting on this, states that it "committed the nation to a crazy-quilt unemployment compensation system, with widely varying benefits distributed under diverging standards." [74] The Committee on Economic Security had tended to agree on the desirability of a national program of unemployment insurance administered federally. However President Roosevelt, influenced perhaps by considerations of what was acceptable to Congress and the danger of an adverse ruling on the constitutionality of a federal system of unemployment insurance, had indicated preference for a state-administered program. [75]

Despite these and other limitations, the main provisions of the

Act constitute a significant break with the past in the attempt to combat the problems of poverty and insecurity, essentially in the provision of a dual system of defense—a public assistance system focusing on immediate relief and a social insurance system aiming at prevention.

Significance of the Social Insurance Provisions

The movement for social insurance played a major role in the enactment of the Social Security Act, specifically the social insurance provisions of the Act. The social insurance provisions represented the nation's response to the demand for long-term solutions to the problem of insecurity in the prevailing socio-economic context. Far from perfect, nevertheless it was the social insurance provisions of the Act that in a real sense signify what has been termed the "the first expression of a changed direction in public policy" in the country. [76]

There was a new understanding of the role of the federal government in national life. This was particularly true in regard to the old-age insurance scheme introduced. The emphasis in social insurance programs was on prevention of need and on providing for likely risks, rather than resort to relief after the individual's poverty had been proved. The right to benefit was also a matter of "earned right," based on the individual's own work and contribution. Apart from individual contributions ensuring more adequate benefits, the arrangement of benefits, being related to contributions in the individual case, made the whole system appear akin to the familiar cooperative self-help program.

There is in the social insurance provisions of the Social Security Act the genius of combining the private insurance principle with the acknowledgment and provision for the federal government's responsibility in social welfare. The concept of insurance against risks through private companies was already there and indigenous to the culture. It therefore, seemed possible to "sell" the concept of social insurance, with emphasis on individual contributions. Eveline Burns,

commenting on the evolution of social insurance, states that it is a "social invention" introduced "to perform a specific function in a specific economic and social environment." She goes on to say:

> It was the ideal instrument for effecting a signficant break in the deterrent treatment of insecure workers, because its apparent analogy with private insurance made the change acceptable to a society which was dominated by business ethics and which stressed individual economic responsibility. [77]

Social insurance is to be viewed as a dynamic social invention having the potential for modifying economic organization and the effects of industrialization. [78] It is in the nature of a sustained and long-term effort to cope with the problems of poverty and insecurity. The debate on the use of government funds for financing social insurance programs in the situation of extreme poverty and need for immediate relief programs—a policy issue even today, particularly in the developing countries—has to be viewed in the context of the potential in social insurance for long-term solutions to the problem of poverty. This is not to justify a policy of ignoring the need for immediate relief to meet human distress, but rather to emphasize the importance of planning and providing for long term programs even as relief programs are under way. Needless to say, this involves some hard thinking and decisions in regard to the optimum use of the limited funds available. It is also important to recognize that despite the potential in social insurance programs for relatively long-term solutions to the problem of poverty—in countries where there is large-scale unemployment over an appreciable period—the stimulation of the economy for greater productivity and increased employment opportunities itself becomes a high priority. It is a dilemma to which social policy makers and statesmen have constantly to address themselves especially in the developing countries.

The social insurance provisions of the Act and the programs that emerged have to be viewed in the context of the opposition and the struggle experienced by the proponents of social insurance in the

preceding decades. Social insurance had been considered a threat to the American way of life and "condemned as an alien importation, if not a foreign conspiracy." The commercial insurance companies and the U.S. Chamber of Commerce continued to misrepresent issues, appealed to fears of "state socialism," and in this way built opposition particularly to compulsory health insurance. [79] Internally, too, the social insurance movement witnessed disagreements and rivalries as seen, for instance, in the relationship between Andrews and Epstein; there was also in the 1930's a growing difference of opinion as to the real purpose of social insurance. In attempting to provide economic security, was the focus to be on prevention of unemployment and employer incentives or on income redistribution? Rubinow and Epstein emphasized the redistribution of income as the main purpose and advocated adequate benefit payments and government leadership in the whole effort. The Social Security Act and its social insurance provisions signify an attempt to reconcile these two differing approaches.

There are also some basic concepts embodied in the social insurance provisions of the Social Security Act of 1935 that are significant and merit consideration. Reference has already been made to the concept of "earned right" of the individual. [80] While this may seem a reactionary approach to the problem of dependency today, it nevertheless signifies progress when seen in relation to the earlier poor law concept of poverty. The right to benefit is viewed as a statutory right which could be enforced by the courts. It is a right based on the individual's work and contribution. Another concept is that of "compulsory coverage," which, it is maintained, is intended to protect the system from "adverse selection of risks as well as to protect the country as a whole against widespread destitution." [81]

There is also the concept of "contributory social insurance, without government subsidy." It is held that the most significant principle in the old-age insurance system introduced by the Social Security Act is that of equal contributions by employers and employees, on a compulsory basis. [82] In contrast to social insurance programs in some other countries, the U.S. program from the time

of its inception has been financed through contributions by employers and employees without resort to any subsidy from the government. [83]

Again, in contrast to social insurance systems in other countries, the Social Security Act emphasized the concept of "wage-related benefits," in the United States. It is pointed out that this is in keeping with a belief that is deeply engrained in American society—that a man's rewards should be in accordance with his own efforts and contributions. [84] In the wage-related principle of benefits, an individual's earnings from employment are said to determine his level of living and the income he is likely to maintain after retirement. However, if the same amount of benefits were paid to each retired worker, the amount would be either so high in the case of some persons that it would be more than their earnings, or it would be so excessively low for others who had higher levels of earning that it would not provide adequate security for them. [85]

These concepts embodied in the social insurance provisions of the Social Security Act of 1935 reflect the nature of the American response to the unprecedented social and economic distress in the country. They are in the nature of a compromise between the earlier laissez faire attitude—the basic commitment to the principles of self-reliance and encouragement of individual initiative—and the demands, emerging from the new situation following the depression, for federal initiative and participation in dealing with the widespread poverty and insecurity.

A Critical Review of the Social Security Act

Reference has already been made to some of the basic provisions of the Social Security Act and to the significance of the social insurance provisions. Some critical comments have already been made in this context. The main focus here, in reviewing the Act, will be its overall significance, how far it really constituted a "changed direction in public policy" and the favorable and the unfavorable reactions to the Act.

The Social Security Act of 1935 has been referred to "as one of the milestones in the history of American social reform." [86] Despite its limitations, it represented the beginning of a "new era of social reform." The temporary and makeshift arrangements to cope with the problem of poverty and distress were replaced by institutional devices that indicated a commitment to long-term solutions in the field of human welfare.

The Social Security Act undoubtedly marked a new direction in public policy. This was evident in the acknowledgement of the federal government's increasing role in social welfare, in the significant transfer of responsibility for welfare from voluntary to public agencies and in the focus on long-term and preventive efforts in combating dependency, notably through social insurance. [87] Apart from acknowledgment of the federal government's permanent responsibility in the field of public dependency and welfare, the manner in which this was effected was also innovative in that it implied a similar commitment in practical terms by the state governments. Essentially, the Act provided the basis for a cooperative effort by government at all levels to deal with long-term socio-economic problems. [88] Ideally there would be a partnership between government and voluntary efforts.

The old shibboleths about government participation in combating dependency and the threat this posed to cherished values of thrift, industry and self-reliance were shattered by the Act. But the Act in no sense signified society's repudiation of these long-held values. As mentioned earlier in discussing the significance of the social insurance provisions, there is in the Social Security Act the genius of combining the private insurance principle based on the value of individual initiative with the feature of federal, state and local participation in social welfare. It has been referred to as a "socialized attack upon the problems of economic insecurity from an essentially individualistic point of view." [89] While industry and thrift were still considered essential for individual security there was the acknowledgment that the individual's work, income and private savings were dependent upon social and economic factors. What the Act did

was to provide "social safeguards" to "supplement the efforts" which individuals would make on their own behalf. [90]

It is important to note that the Social Security Act, while signifying a "break with inhibitions of the past" and pointing to new directions in public policy, was in no sense a complete departure from the earlier traditions. While it established the fact that each individual had social rights, it did not assert for instance "that government owes every man a living," as was feared in certain quarters. The objective in dealing with dependency, however, revealed a significant break with the traditions of the poor law in the Act's emphasis on self-respect, encouragement of self-support and preventive work. Certainly there was no precedent to the insurance provisions that were ushered in by the Act—the operation of social insurance by the government on a nonprofit basis. [91]

The Social Security Act was criticized by both liberals and conservatives. Liberals expressed disappointment that the Act failed to cover all workers and that its benefit payments were inadequate. The American Association of Social Workers had supported the passage of the Act, but they had advocated federal assistance to the states to meet not only the needs of the elderly and dependent children, but all persons in need. [92] Social workers were critical of what appeared to be an arbitrary way in which certain groups were provided for and others not. Frank Bruno, writing on the "Social Work Aspects of the Social Security Act," in 1936 stated:

> Our Act . . . picks out certain beneficiaries and ignores others in what seems wholly an arbitrary manner, e.g., the crippled child is pointedly indicated for good and potentially adequate care; the child with heart disease by any one of a number of troubles is passed by.
>
> . . . Social workers are coming to be very critical of any provision for special classes, even though such classes may be determined by medical diagnosis. Contrariwise, social workers feel that the only just method for approaching problems of dependency is to handle them as dependents, not as special classes, as folks who

for some reason cannot support themselves not because they happen to be widows, or unemployed. [93]

The criticism was not only in regard to the exclusion of some groups and the favored treatment of others, but also pertaining to the whole approach of categorical relief.

Economists tended to criticize the Act on the grounds that the payroll taxes were deflationary. Employers protested the additional tax burdens. [94] In fact some of the employer groups, such as the National Association of Manufacturers and the Ohio Chamber of Commerce, opposed the legislation. [95] Among the conservatives, the business leaders, even prior to the passage of the Act, had expressed fears that with unemployment insurance there would be a large number who would prefer not to work, that with old-age insurance the virtue of saving would disappear—that moral degradation seemed inevitable. This point of view was represented in the extreme by Republican Congressman John Taber who stated:

Never in the history of the world has any measure been brought in here so insidiously designed as to prevent business recovery, to enslave workers, and to prevent any possibility of the employers providing work for the people. [96]

The Social Security Act was also criticized by leaders from within the social insurance movement, notably Epstein and Rubinow. Epstein was the most persistent and uncompromising critic, who pointed to the failure of the Act to effect any significant redistribution in income. Writing on "Our Social Insecurity Act" in 1935, Epstein held that due to the many failings of the Act, such as the lack of government contributions, the bill, "instead of bringing about social security, may actually secure for American nothing but continuous insecurity." [97] Rubinow, too, criticized the Act for the token redistribution of incomes, the failure to introduce health insurance—in short for not going far in the effort to provide social security.

Scholars commenting on the Act have also pointed to its serious limitations, stating that in many respects it was "an astonishingly inept and conservative piece of legislation." They also noted that in hardly any other welfare system in the world was there the feature of the state avoiding responsibility for the situation of poverty in old-age and resorting to compulsory payments from current earnings. The Act, they held, not only failed to provide a national system of unemployment compensation, but also satisfactory national standards. [98] These and other limitations, such as the failure to provide health insurance, indicate that the Act is far from complete.

Despite these shortcomings, the Social Security Act was hailed as providing the means for a sounder democracy and an opportunity for the social work profession to assume leadership in constructive social welfare administration. Arthur Schlesinger, commenting in the same vein, states that with the Social Security Act of 1935 "the constitutional dedication of federal power to general welfare began a new phase of national history." [99]

The Act and its provisions are to be viewed as an important attempt, at a point in the social welfare history of the country, to reconcile the demands of justice, security and freedom. The policies and programs embodied in the Act emerged as a compromise in the context of opposing philosophies, pressures of interest groups and differing viewpoints. As mentioned earlier within the social insurance movement itself, there were differing interpretations as to the basic purpose of social insurance. One point of view, the chief spokesmen of which were Andrews and Commons, emphasized prevention of unemployment and the provision of employer incentives, as the main purpose. As opposed to this view, Rubinow and Epstein persistently pointed to redistribution of income as the essential goal of social insurance. The Act is to be seen as an attempt to reconcile these differing approaches within the social insurance movement and outside—to arrive at the most feasible solution at a given time in a particular context.

No one event, individual, or system of thought determined exclusively the shape or substance of the policies and programs intro-

duced by the Act. However, the Great Depression of the 1930's was in a real sense the immediately precipitating factor in the passage of the Act. While the depression and the unprecedented social and economic distress dramatized the urgency for government intervention, the nature of the national response to the crisis and the long-term solutions attempted, culminating in the Act, were influenced considerably by the leadership exercised by President Roosevelt and his advisers, and the pressure for change exerted by the respective reform movements.

The Social Security Act, which the President himself referred to as the "cornerstone of his administration," ushered in by the New Deal, signified in a very real sense a change in public policy. The subsequent amendments to the Act represent further progress in the reform effort to extend social insurance and assistance to more people, to liberalize benefits and to raise pertinent policy issues in the ongoing task of making society and government more responsive to the social and economic needs of all people.

NOTES

1. Arthur J. Altmeyer. *The Formative Years of Social Security.* Madison: University of Wisconsin Press, 1966, p. 6.

2. Richard Hofstadter. *Social Darwinism in American Thought.* Boston: Beacon Press, 1967. pp. 6-7. Note: Hofstadter points out that Social Darwinism as a conservative philosophy lacked many of the important characteristics of conservatism, despite its defense of the status quo and the attack on social reform.

3. *Ibid.,* p. 203.

4. Philip Klein. *From Philanthropy to Social Welfare.* San Francisco: Jossey-Bass, Inc., 1968, p. 270.

5. Frederick L. Allen, "Economic Security: A Look Back and a Look Ahead," in William Haber and Wilbur Cohen, eds. *Social Security: Programs, Problems and Policies,* Homewood, Ill.: Richard D. Irwin, Inc., 1960 p. 32.

6. Oscar Handlin, "Foreword" in Roy Lubove, *The Struggle for Social Security 1900-1935,* Cambridge, Mass.: Harvard University Press, 1968, p. vii.

7. John C. Kidneigh. "The Welfare State: What Is It?" in *The Welfare State, Menace or Millenium?* presented and published under the auspices of the Social Science Research Center of the Graduate School, University of Minnesota, 1950, p. 9.

8. U.S. Committee on Economic Security, *Social Security in America: the Factual Background of the Social Security Act as Summarized from Staff*

Reports to the Committee on Economic Security, Social Security Board, Washington, D.C.: U.S. Government Printing Office, 1937, p. 158.

9. Roy Lubove. *The Struggle for Social Security 1900-1935.* Cambridge, Mass.: Harvard University Press, 1968, p. 2.

10. *Ibid.,* p. 3.

11. See Charles E. Jacob. *Policy and Bureaucracy,* New York: D. Van Nostrand Company, Inc., 1966, p. 20. Note: If has been argued that the successful refutation of the philosophy of "negative government" was the lasting contribution of the intellectual leaders of the Progressive era. Nevertheless, the earlier theories continued to exercise influence.

12. U.S. Committee on Economic Security, *op. cit.,* pp. 139 and 260. Note: The birthrate showed an increasing trend from the 1940's onwards.

13. Lubove, *op. cit.,* p. 114.

14. U.S. Committee on Economic Security, *op. cit.,* p. 143.

15. *Ibid.,* p. 260.

16. *Ibid.,* p. 265.

17. See Elizabeth C. Tandy. *Comparability of Maternal Mortality Rates in the United States and Certain Foreign Countries.* Children's Bureau Publication No. 229, U.S. Department of Labor. Washington, D.C.: U.S. Government Printing Office, 1935.

18. See President's Research Committee on Social Trends, *Recent Social Trends in the United States.* Vol. I. New York: McGraw-Hill Book Co., 1933, pp. 325-381; gives fuller account of the educational system prior to the depression of the 1930's.

19. See President's Research Committee on Social Trends, *op. cit.,* pp. 325-381.

20. John D. Hogan and Francis A. J. Ianni. *American Social Legislation.* New York: Harper & Brothers, 1956, p. 496.

21. Altmeyer, *op. cit.,* p. 9.

22. Arthur M. Schlesinger, Jr., *The Coming of the New Deal.* Boston: Houghton Mifflin Company, 1958, p. 294.

23. *Ibid.,* p. 2.

24. Corning, *op. cit.,* p. 28.

25. Robert H. Bremner. *From the Depths.* New York: New York University Press, 1956, p. 260.

26. Hogan and Ianni, *op. cit.,* p. 494.

27. President's Research Committee on Social Trends, *op. cit.,* p. lxxi.

28. *Ibid.,* p. lxxi.

29. *Ibid.,* pp. lxxiv-lxxv.

30. Frederick L. Allen. "Economic Security: A Look Back and a Look Ahead," in Haber and Cohen, *op. cit.,* p. 34.

31. Charles I. Schottland. *The Social Security Program in the United States.* New York: Appleton-Century-Crofts, 1963, p. 30.

32. Bremner, *op. cit.,* p. 261. Note: While Hoover's efforts to meet the problems of the depression were delayed and inadequate, scholars attach significance to the very decision that the business cycle was subject to man's control, and his inauguration of programs to control the cycle. This in itself, despite the failure of his programs, is viewed as an advance and a significant change. See Albert U. Romasco, *The Poverty of Abundance: Hoover, the Nation, the Depression,* London: Oxford University Press, 1965, pp. 230-234.

33. Altmeyer, *op. cit.,* p. 9. See also, Carl N. Degler, "Introduction," in *The New Deal,* Carl N. Degler, ed. Chicago: Quadrangle Books, 1970, pp. 3-4.

34. Schottland, *op. cit.*, p. 23.

35. Lubove, *op. cit.*, p. 25.

36. Corning, *op. cit.*, pp. 6-7.

37. Lubove, *op. cit.*, pp. 29-30. Note: Andrews' leadership continued until his death in 1943.

38. *Ibid.*, p. 113.

39. Schottland, *op. cit.*, p. 26.

40. See Clarke A. Chambers. *Seedtime of Reform*. Ann Arbor: The University of Michigan Press, 1967, p. 219; Roy Lubove, *op. cit.*, p. 114.

41. *Ibid.*, p. 26.

42. Francis Brown, "Three 'Pied Pipers' of the Depression," Carl N. Degler, ed., *The New Deal*. Chicago: Quadrangle Books, 1970, p. 69.

43. Degler, *op. cit.*, p. 8.

44. Altmeyer, *op. cit.*, p. 10.

45. It should be noted that the main objective initially of the American Association of Social Workers, founded in 1917, was to ensure professional standards for social work. Individual social workers in collaboration with social reformers were, however, active in the cause of social insurance.

46. See Chambers, *op. cit.*; Irving Bernstein. *The Lean Years*. Baltimore: Penguin Books, 1966; Blanche D. Coll. *Perspectives in Public Welfare*. Office of Research, Demonstration and Training, Intramural Research Division, Social and Rehabilitation Service, Washington, D.C.: U.S. Government Printing Office, 1970, p. 87.

47. See Chambers, *op. cit.*, p. 223; Altmeyer, *op. cit.*, pp. 32-33. Note: The American Federation of Labor did play an important part in the later stages of the bill, especially in regard to the "Clark amendment," doing its best to ensure passage of the bill.

48. *Ibid.*, p. 266.

49. Corning, *op. cit.*, p. 25.

50. Chambers, *op. cit.*, pp. 215-218.

51. Hogan and Ianni, *op. cit.*, p. 70.

52. Richard Hofstadter. *The Age of Reform*. New York: Random House, Vintage Books, 1955, pp. 302-304.

53. Degler, *op. cit.*, p. 16.

54. Morton Keller, ed., "The Clash of Contemporaries," *The New Deal*. New York: Holt, Rinehart & Winston, 1963, p. 6.

55. Degler, *op. cit.*, p. 16.

56. Altmeyer, *op. cit.*, p. 9.

57. Degler, *op. cit.*, p. 150.

58. *Ibid.*

59. U.S. Congress, House Committee on Ways and Means. *The Social Security Bill: Report to Accompany H.R. 7260 (H. Rept. 615, 74th Cong; 1st sess.)* Washington, D.C.: U.S. Government Printing Office, 1935, p. 2.

60. Altmeyer, *op. cit.*, p. 7.

61. U.S. Committee on Economic Security, *op. cit.*, Preface, iii.

62. Altmeyer, *op. cit.*, p. 15.

63. *Basic Questions of Policy on which Early Decisions Are Deemed Very Necessary, August 11, 1934*, Committee on Economic Security, General, National Archives, Record Group 47, Washington, D.C.

64. Altmeyer, *op. cit.*, p. 16.

65. *Ibid.* See also: Schottland, *op. cit.*, p. 36.

66. Hogan and Ianni, *op. cit.*, p. 499.

67. Schottland, *op. cit.*, p. 38.

68. Hogan and Ianni, *op. cit.*, p. 502.

69. *Ibid.*

70. U.S. Committee on Economic Security, *op. cit.*, p. 222.

71. *Ibid.*, p. 224.

72. Joseph G. Rayback. *A History of American Labor.* New York: The Free Press, 1966, pp. 338-339.

73. Gaston V. Rimlinger. "American Social Security in A European Perspective," William G. Bowen, *et al*, eds. *The American System of Social Insurance: Its Philosophy, Impact, and Future Development.* New York: McGraw-Hill Book Company, 1968, p. 226.

74. Schlesinger, *op. cit.*, p. 313.

75. Schottland, *op. cit.*, pp. 79-80.

76. Wilbur J. Cohen. "Federalism and Social Insurance," Bowen, *et al, op. cit.*, p. 1.

77. Eveline M. Burns. "Social Security: Social Insurance in Evolution," *American Economic Review*, Vol. XXXIV, No. 1, Part 2, March 1944, p. 199.

78. *Ibid.*

79. Lubove, *op. cit.*, p. 6.

80. See Chapter 1.

81. Schottland, *op. cit.*, p. 67.

82. Douglas J. Brown, "Old-Age Insurance Under the Social Security Act," *National Municipal Review*, Vol. XXV, No. 3, March 1936, p. 3.

83. Schottland, *op. cit.*, p. 58.

84. *Ibid.*, p. 68.

85. *Ibid.*

86. Bremner, *op. cit.*, p. 264.

87. Lubove, *op. cit.*, p. 179.

88. Edwin E. Witte. "Social Security A Wild Dream or a Practical Plan," in *Social Security Perspectives*, Robert J. Lampman, ed. Madison: The University of Wisconsin Press, 1962, p. 6.

89. *Ibid.*, p. 12.

90. *Ibid.*, p. 13.

91. *Ibid.*, p. 10.

92. Altmeyer, *op. cit.*, p. 33.

93. Frank J. Bruno. "Social Work Aspects of the Social Security Act," in *The Heritage of American Social Work.* eds. Ralph and Muriel Pumphrey. New York: Columbia University Press, 1964, p. 444.

94. Rayback, *op. cit.*, p. 340.

95. Altmeyer, *op. cit.*, p. 33.

96. Schlesinger, *op. cit.*, p. 311.

97. Abraham Epstein. "Our Social Insecurity Act," *Harper's Magazine*, Harper & Brothers Publishers, December 1935, p. 66.

98. William E. Leuchtenberg. Franklin D. *Roosevelt and the New Deal.* New York: Harper and Row, 1965, p. 132.

99. Schlesinger, *op. cit.*, p. 315.

III

Basic Policy Changes in Social Insurance in Social Security Act Amendments, 1935–1954

> The social problem must, as long as societies continue to endure, be solved afresh by almost every generation; and the one chance of progress depends both upon an invincible loyalty to a constructive social ideal and upon a correct understanding by the new generation of the actual experience of its predecessors.
>
> Herbert Croly, *The Promise of American Life.* (The Macmillan Company, © 1912.)

Policy Issues in the Amendments to the Act

IN SIGNING the Social Security Act of 1935, President Franklin D. Roosevelt referred to it as "a cornerstone in a structure which is being built, but is by no means complete." [1] The Act in no sense represented a set of policies and programs in social insurance and public assistance that were complete or final. It marked the first step in an "evolutionary process." There followed several amendments to the Social Security Act in the course of which policy issues were raised and changes made in the light of new demands and criticism. While these amendments have reflected changes in social insurance and public assistance, for the most part changes in public assistance have been minor. It is in the social insurance features of the Act that there have been more basic policy issues raised and changes made.

The focus here will be on policy issues in social insurance, as reflected in the amendments to the Social Security Act of 1935 in 1939, 1946, 1950, 1952 and 1954. There will be particular emphasis on issues pertaining to old-age insurance, survivors' insurance and disability insurance.

The passage of the Social Security Act of 1935 did not signify an end to the forces opposed to the social security movement. Even well-wishers of the program doubted whether the constitutionality of the Act would be upheld by the courts. However, in May 1937 the United States Supreme Court upheld the constitutionality of both the unemployment insurance and old-age insurance features of the Social Security Act. Justice Cardozo in upholding the old-age insurance provisions of the Act made the following historic statement, emphasizing the need for a national approach, and for policies and programs responsive to changing conditions:

Nor is the concept of the general welfare static. Needs that were narrow or parochial a century ago may be interwoven in our

day with the well-being of the nation. What is critical or urgent changes with the times.

He went on to state that the problem is "plainly national in area and dimensions." [2]

The Court's decision upholding the constitutionality of the Act gave the impetus to a movement for liberalization of the provisions of the Social Security Act.

But there were still differing views as to the objectives of Social Security. Consequently, differing policies were advocated and policy issues raised in the amendments to the Act of 1935. [3]

(1) There was the Administration's view—the view of the Social Security Board and those associated with it. They saw the basic objective of social security as one of ensuring the "economic essentials" to all people faced with the personal exingencies of life. It did not imply full governmental responsibility for the security of individuals at all times, but rather the provision of essentials of life when the individual faced adverse circumstances beyond his control. The responsibility for his own support and that of the family was still primarily that of the individual. However, in personal contingencies such as old-age, sickness, disability and unemployment, where the individual is helpless due to circumstances beyond his control, social security is intended to provide support.

(2) There were right-wing critics who argued that the government should not undertake responsibility in areas that could be dealt with by voluntary effort. They maintained that private social security institutions are preferable to governmental programs. This was an effort, if possible, to turn the clock back, and appealed exclusively to the principles of private enterprise and voluntary effort.

(3) There were others, also right wing critics, who sought to restrict the scope of Social Security to public assistance and vocational rehabilitation. If possible they would attempt to elimi-

nate social insurance programs and restrict the use of the term "insurance" to the different types of private insurance.

(4) Another group, which included many Keynesian economists, approached Social Security from the point of view of its total effects on the economy. Social Security was viewed more as an instrument or a tool for stabilizing the economy rather than meeting individual and family needs. Altmeyer refers to a heated dialogue with a U.S. Treasury economist who represented this point of view, which is interesting and revealing. There were basic policy questions at issue—whether the social insurance scheme was to be financed out of general revenues and used primarily as an instrument for stabilizing the economy, or whether the principle of contributory social insurance and the arrangement of wage-related benefits should continue. The economist was more interested in using Social Security as a device to stabilize the economy, than for the intended beneficiaries of the scheme.

The dialogue, which is an interesting revelation of differing values, attitudes and priorities in policy consideration, is reported to have gone as follows:

> Just what do you mean by a flat pension?
> A pension geared to the business cycle.
> Well, what do you mean by that?
> What we mean is that, when we're in a slump, we step up the flat pension, and when we have inflation threatening us, we cut back.
> What kind of a social program would that be; where would you get any security for the individual out of a program like that?
> We don't give a damn about how it's done as long as you shovel out the money when it's needed to iron out the business cycle.
> Don't you think there is any value in relating benefits and contributions to wages?
> That's just a lot of—(an obscene expression that cannot be recorded). [4]

(5) There were also adherents to a more radical view who saw

in Social Security the basic purpose of redistribution of income. Abraham Epstein and Isaac Rubinow, who played an important role in the move to liberalize the Social Security Act, emphasized the importance of government contributions in ensuring substantial redistribution of incomes.

Inevitably, these and other differing views as to the objectives of Social Security meant varying approaches to the policy issues that arose in the amendments to the Social Security Act of 1935. The amendments to the Act, like the Act of 1935 itself, represent compromises at given points in time in the American effort to deal with the problem of insecurity and poverty, and to extend protection against risks.

A persistent policy issue to which the several amendments to the Social Security Act of 1935 had to address themselves was the determination of an appropriate level of benefit payments. It involved the question of the adequacy of social insurance benefits in the context of changing needs and conditions. This continues to be a key issue even today. Compromises have to be made between adequacy and equity, and there are related considerations such as methods of funding and the particular stage in the economic development of the country. The level of adequacy that seems appropriate at one stage changes as national productivity and general standards of living increase. Hence, the social adequacy of the benefit payments becomes a changing problem to which each new generation has to address itself in its particular context. [5]

Related to the issue of social adequacy was the question as to whether benefits should be the same for all persons or wage-related, as determined by the Social Security Act. Despite the Townsend Movement and its agitation for equal and universal payments, the amendments to the Act upheld the original concept of wage-related benefits. The policy of paying differential benefits based on wages has several objectives, such as ensuring the workers' motivation for making the optimum contribution, and relating benefits to different

economic situations. [6] But there is the basic question as to how far social insurance, providing benefits related to wages, can be adequate when wages themselves are inadequate to certain groups or, in the context of built-in structural unemployment, where four to five percent of the working population may inevitably have to be unemployed or in and out of work. The several amendments to the Act of 1935 have not provided a satisfactory answer to this problem. It has been argued, in this context, that even if there is an adequate social insurance scheme it will still be necessary to have a satisfactory and humane system of public assistance.

Another related policy issue is that of the method of financing social security programs. The Act of 1935 and the subsequent amendments had to consider the question whether the Social Security program should be financed by employer-employee contributions or by general taxes. This again is a recurring question. The Act and the amendments upheld the principle of joint employer-employee contribution, without resort to general taxes. There are some countries, however, with the contributory insurance system in which the government also make a contribution. It is also interesting that the contributory principle is gaining acceptance in countries that had earlier hesitated to adopt this principle or had embraced it only partially.

There have been strong arguments advanced to amend the Social Security Act to provide for government contributions and for using the social security system as a means for substantial redistribution of income—notably by Epstein. Opponents of this view maintain that substantial government contributions would weaken the concept of benefit as earned right. They also point to possibility of a means test and benefit payments barely above the subsistence level. [7] But the question arises, is it fair to insist in all instances on joint contribution by worker and employer on the principle of wage-related benefits? What if the wages themselves are inadequate? Are there some groups whose circumstances justify government contributions on a temporary or long-term basis? These policy issues will continue

to be raised in approaching the difficult task of ensuring adequate benefit payments for all within the framework of a wage-related benefit system.

Another significant policy issue that the different amendments to the Social Security Act had to consider was that of extending coverage to new groups and the basis for such extension. (The Act of 1935 had failed, for example, to extend coverage to several groups of workers, especially those who needed protection most, such as farm laborers and domestic workers.) Administrative, financial, constitutional and other basic questions were involved in this issue.

Compulsory insurance was still another policy issue confronting the policy makers associated with the Act of 1935 and its amendments. This was upheld as an important aspect of the Social Security program. Yet in the case of the physicians—a powerful political pressure group—allowance was made for their staying out of the scheme altogether. In this connection it is pointed out that the resistance of such groups as the self-employed physicians should not be permitted to determine whether they should be included or excluded, when others are compelled to adhere to the system. [8] Exclusion was also applied specifically to certain other groups, such as employees of nonprofit religious, educational and charitable organizations, in the 1950 and 1954 amendments to the Act.

There were other policy issues, such as benefit provisions for survivors and dependents, that the Act of 1935 had failed to resolve and that were to be debated and decided upon in the amendments of 1939. However, resistance by the American Medical Association, employers' organizations and casualty insurance companies successfully thwarted any substantial move to introduce disability insurance benefits during the 1935-1954 period.

The Concept of Family Protection in the 1939 Amendments

The Social Security Administration's built-in requirement of research and recommendation of changes for improvement in the provisions of the Act helped considerably in the periodic task of

drafting amendments to the Act of 1935. As the provisions of the Act were implemented, bringing increased administrative experience and understanding of the real needs of people, as well as additional data and feedbacks, changes to the Act were bound to be introduced. The momentum for such change came from both within and outside the administration. In the administration, the Social Security Board and its Chairman, Arthur J. Altmeyer, and other closely associated officials played a significant role. [9] The social reform movements and the social reformers constituted an "outside force," pressing for changes in policies and programs.

There were several limitations in the provisions of the Social Security Act of 1935, necessitating changes, which became more evident as the programs were developed. The Act did not cover dependents and survivors. The emphasis had been on the individual worker and his joint contribution from his earnings in providing for his security in old age—as a matter of "earned right." The focus was mainly on "individual protection" rather than "family protection." What kind of protection did this offer the members of the family? In the event of the breadwinner's death, for example, the survivors were left unprovided for. The unemployment insurance Titles of the Act revealed a basic flaw—there was no minimum standard specified that the states had to adhere to. There were also the several categories excluded under the unemployment insurance scheme, such as agricultural workers, workers engaged in domestic service, and charitable and educational workers. This exclusion limited unemployment coverage to approximately 22,000,000 working men—less than half the gainfully employed persons. [10] Even in the case of those who were covered under the unemployment and old-age insurance schemes, the benefit payments allowed were inadequate. These and other limitations gave rise to a movement for the liberalization of the Act, leading to the first important amendment in 1939.

A fair amount of the initiative for the policy changes in the 1939 and subsequent amendments came from the Social Security Board and its dedicated and competent staff. In this, Arthur J. Altmeyer as Chairman of the Social Security Board played an important role. It

should also be noted that President Roosevelt himself took a personal interest in the movement for liberalizing the Act. In a letter to Altmeyer, written on April 28, 1938, the President reiterated his concern for improving and extending the provisions:

The successful operation of the Act is the best proof that it was soundly conceived. However, it would be unfortunate if we assumed that it was complete and final. Rather, we should be constantly seeking to perfect and strengthen it in the light of our accumulating experience and growing appreciation of social needs.

I am particularly anxious that the Board give attention to the development of a sound plan for liberalizing the old-age insurance system. In the development of such a plan, I should like to have the board give consideration to the feasibility of extending its coverage, . . . paying larger benefits than now provided in the Act for those retiring during the earlier years of the system, providing benefits for aged wives and widows, and providing benefits for young children of insured persons dying before reaching retirement age. [11]

The President in conclusion expressed the hope that the Board would be able to submit its recommendations before Congress reconvened in January 1939.

Social Security policies and the question of amendments to the Act became national issues, receiving careful attention in Congress. Policies affecting the lives of millions of people were certain to be reexamined and debated nationally. Indeed the Democratic and Republic platforms of 1936 and their respective Social Security planks had already indicated the need for changes in the Act of 1935. The two parties' approaches to Social Security, however, varied.

Social Security had become a major issue in the election campaign in 1936. The Republican candidate, Governor Landon, in a speech at Milwaukee attacked the Social Security Act as "unjust,

unworkable, stupidly drafted and wastefully financed." He went on to say:

> And to call it "Social Security" is a fraud on the working man. . . . The saving it forces on our workers is a cruel hoax. . . . To get a workable old-age pension plan, we must repeal the present compulsory insurance plan. The Republican Party is pledged to do this. [12]

Social Security was still very much a partisan issue and the existing program was identified for the most part with the Democratic party. Democrats made no secret of it. The election leaflets issued by the Democratic National Campaign Committee in 1936 stated that old-age insurance was the right of every worker—"Democrats gave it to you—Don't let Republicans take it away." [13]

The Democratic platform of 1936 made specific reference to the "protection of the family and the home," which in a sense fore-shadowed what was to come under the amendments of 1939—the inclusion of survivors and dependents benefits. Old-age and Social Security programs were viewed as an important means to the attainment of the objective of "family protection." Included in the Democratic platform's old-age and Social Security plank in 1936 was the following statement of policy:

> We have built foundations for the security of those who are faced with the hazards of unemployment and old-age; for the orphaned, the crippled and the blind. On the foundation of the Social Security Act we are determined to erect a structure of economic security for all our people, making sure that this benefit shall keep step with the ever-increasing capacity of America to provide a high standard of living for all its citizens. [14]

There was also included in that 1936 platform a merit system plank which was to have an important bearing on the Social Security programs, in ensuring the development of a more enlightened and

efficient administration—a plank for which the national League of Women Voters had campaigned actively for inclusion in the platforms of all political parties in 1936. Likewise, the American Association of Social Workers and other concerned groups denounced the spoils system and advocated the establishment of a merit system. The efforts of these groups for the inclusion of the merit system plank undoubtedly contributed to the specific provision in the amendments of 1939 for a state personnel merit system.

While the initiative for changes in the Social Security Act, to an appreciable extent, came from within the administration, the role of the reform movements and the reformers and the pressure and leadership exercised by them should not be underestimated. Undoubtedly, the extent of influence exercised and the resources at their command for rallying support for their objectives varied among the reform movements.

In the amendments of 1939, the Townsend Movement, the labor movement and the American Association for Social Security under Epstein exerted the greatest outside pressure. Other groups, such as the League of Women Voters, the National Consumers' League, and the American Association of Social Workers, also made representations for specific changes with which they were particularly concerned. It was, however, the labor movement (which initially had been slow to support the cause of the social insurance movement) that was to play an increasingly significant role in the extension of Social Security benefits in the 1939 and subsequent amendments.

The Advisory Council on Social Security appointed jointly in 1937 by the Special Committee on Social Security of the Senate Finance Committee and the Social Security Board—which made specific recommendations regarding amendments to the Social Security Act—included representatives of labor organizations, employers' organizations and other members of the public. The terms of reference of the Advisory Council were sufficiently broad to include important policy questions, such as the advisability of extending benefits to groups hitherto excluded, inclusion of survivors' benefits,

increasing the size of monthly benefits and the size, character and disposition of reserves. [15]

The Advisory Council played an active and influential role in pushing for changes in the Act and in making the concept of family protection a reality through the amendments of 1939. Arthur Altmeyer, as Chairman of the Social Security Board, utilized skillfully the Advisory Council and the reformers and interest groups represented in it to further the movement for constructive changes. Efforts were also made to use prevailing adverse winds constructively for this purpose. In addition to Arthur Altmeyer, Douglas Brown and Edwin Witte, there were such other reformers as Eveline Burns and Abraham Epstein who, as either close associates or persistent critics, made a vital contribution in the push for change and liberalization of the Social Security program.

Epstein was a persistent critic of the 1935 Act, from outside the administration. The 1939 amendments, it is reported, "testified to the validity" of several of the criticisms made by Epstein. [16] He had stressed the principle of social adequacy in social insurance. The Social Security Act had embodied a combination of the principles of equity and adequacy. To provide for at least a minimum of social adequacy the Act of 1935 had deviated from the equity principle that is implicit in the contributory contractual system. [17] But the main emphasis was on the equity principle and this, Epstein protested, was no social insurance. He also pointed to several other limitations of the Act, notably the lack of provision for dependents' and survivors' allowances.

In a statement presented before the Advisory Council on Social Security on December 10, 1937, Epstein criticized strongly the limitations of the Act and urged that constructive amendments be introduced:

> As I see it, the underlying defect of the present program of old-age insurance embodied in the Act lies in the fact that although intended as a social-insurance measure, it completely violates what has been known as social insurance for the past 50

years. . . . In social insurance it matters little whether the people bearing the risk pay the contributions themselves. What is of prime concern is that those who suffer most should receive the greatest protection. Since its chief aim is to accomplish socially desirable ends, the premium rates are dictated by social policy, not by the actuary. [18]

This lack of protection for dependents and survivors and the inadequate benefits payable to those covered was to Epstein unthinkable in a program that was termed "social insurance." There were other individuals and groups, notably the Townsend Movement and its spokesmen, who expressed dissatisfaction with the Act's provisions, and the need for more adequate protection. Undoubtedly the Advisory Council on Social Security had a close relationship with the Social Security Board and in a very real sense each influenced the other, with the Board Chairman playing a key role. The Social Security Board submitted its report on December 30, 1938, indicating to the President and Congress the changes it would recommend in the Social Security Act. There were changes recommended in regard to old-age insurance, unemployment insurance, public assistance and health.

It is significant that President Roosevelt in transmitting the recommendations of the Board to Congress on January 16, 1939 endorsed all its major recommendations. In the hearings of the House Ways and Means Committee many bills introduced to amend the Social Security Act were considered.

Representatives of the different reform movements appeared before that Committee to press for their schemes and recommendations. The fact that over fifty Representatives and two Senators, testified on behalf of the Townsend Movement indicated its strength. [19] The amendments of 1939, like the Social Security Act of 1935 itself, were furthered by the threat of more radical changes posed by the Townsend and related old-age pension schemes. Dr. Townsend in his testimony before the House Ways and Means Committee stated:

As far as the social security legislation that we have now, that is the height of absurdity, of all legislation that has ever been passed by this Congress, in my estimation. Let us do away with it.

He went on to indicate the changes that he would favor:

I believe we should have immediately a constitutional amendment calling for a blanket annuity insurance for every citizen of the United States without discrimination, without a means test applied.

For the money to support that retirement annuity for the aged, let us exact that by having everybody help to buy the retirement annuity by paying throughout their productive careers a certain percentage of the pay that they get for what they sell. [20]

The radical scheme proposed by the Townsendites, and the extent of support they seemed to have, no doubt impelled substantial changes of the original Act. Dr. Abraham Epstein, Executive Secretary of the American Association for Social Security, was among others who also appeared before the House Ways and Means Committee, with a view to exerting pressure for changes. "The earlier concept of relief as a punishment for poverty," Epstein argued, could no longer be held and "must be substituted by the concept of social protection." He went on to say:

Concretely, what I mean is that the benefits established under the social security program must provide for at least a minimum of subsistence in accordance with the needs of the family, . . .

In both old-age insurance and unemployment insurance you have got to get accustomed to the idea that government must make a contribution. [21]

The concept of "family protection" was implied in Epstein's statement. But he was pushing for changes more fundamental than this—he was advocating the use of social insurance as a means of redistributing income with the aid of government subsidy.

Several representatives of labor testified before the House Committee. Mathew Woll, representing the American Federation of Labor, endorsed the recommendations of the Advisory Council on Social Security. Woll went further in his demands than had the Advisory Council and urged coverage of all farm workers and employees of charitable organizations. Commenting also on policy regarding extensions in Social Security coverage and improvements in standards, Woll stated:

The American Federation of Labor believes that the policy of extensions in coverages and improvements in standards should be formulated by Congress in such a manner that each agency concerned has a unified function to perform . . . To approve or disapprove proposed amendments separately without seeing their effect on the entire policy of social security is to build a patchwork structure . . . [22]

Representatives of labor, and the labor movement in general, thus gave increasing support to the cause of liberalizing the provisions of the Act, leading to the amendments of 1939. There was a continuing effort by labor, obviously motivated to a large extent by the benefits that would accrue to wage earners themselves, but nevertheless humane and sustained, helping to bring about necessary changes. This sustained effort manifested itself in different forms, notably in policy statements issued at the annual conventions, in the participation of labor representatives in the deliberations of the Advisory Council on Social Security, and in testimony before Congressional Committees. There were also efforts made to contact individual members of the House Ways and Means Committee and the Senate Finance Committee to influence their thinking, while the amendments to the Social Security Act were being discussed in Congress.

Labor's efforts to influence policy changes in social insurance and to push for the amendments of 1939 not only involved lobbying and related activity, but also such educational efforts as policy statements at annual conventions and periodic press releases, indicating to the public the policy issues in social insurance as seen by labor,

and seeking support for the changes that labor sought to introduce by way of amendment to the Social Security Act.

Representatives of the American Association of Social Workers also testified before the House Ways and Means Committee indicating the association's and social workers' position in regard to the Social Security Act, and proposing amendments to the Act. William Hodson, in presenting the AASW views, stated:

> ... I should like to say on behalf of the social workers of the country that we believe the Social Security Act, which was passed in 1935, marks the greatest step forward which this country has taken in the field of public welfare throughout its entire history. ... However, the social workers of the country believe that we should look upon the Social Security Act as sound in principles, but experimental in operation. From time to time it needs change and amendment in the light of our experience and in the light of the needs of the people of this country. [23]

Emphasizing the need for the introduction of the merit system in public welfare administration, Hodson added:

> Civil service and the merit system alone can provide that measure of efficiency in governmental service which will make the democratic system work.

Hodson was pushing for a change that social work had constantly emphasized, and which was closely related to the AASW goal of ensuring professional standards in social work.

There is no doubt that this kind of support for the recommendations of the Social Security Board regarding Act amendments, given by the different reform movements including social work in Congressional hearings and in public statements, provided considerable help to the movement for liberalizing the Act via the 1939 amendments.

The efforts made by AASW and social work generally in this cause, when viewed apart from that of the rest of the reform movements, seemed to be lacking, relatively, in strength and suste-

nance. However it should be noted that AASW and Social workers in general did not place great emphasis on lobbying activity and influencing policy changes in legislation during this period. The main concern, particularly in the early stages, was that of ensuring professional standards for social work. Nevertheless, social work's efforts constituted an integral part of the total effort by the reform movements for policy changes leading to the 1939 amendments.

The Social Security Act was amended on August 10, 1939 to include, under old-age and survivors' insurance, protection for dependents and survivors. There were to be dependent benefits payable to the wife and young children of retired workers and survivor benefits payable to the widow, orphans and dependent parents of deceased workers who had been insured. The title of the old-age insurance system established under the Social Security Act was changed to Old-Age and Survivors' Insurance (called "OASI"). The new pattern of benefit introduced was characterized as "family protection," different from the earlier "individual protection." It had the distinct social advantage of relating benefits payable to probable need as indicated by the existence of dependents. It was also in keeping with the prevailing societal values of keeping the family intact; survivors' and dependents' insurance was viewed as a tool for furthering this goal. [24]

The amendments of 1939 were a response, however limited, to some of the basic criticisms of the Act that were affirmed by the Advisory Council on Social Security. Following the 1939 amendments, the "rigid actuarial relation" between contributions and benefits that had prevailed under the original provisions of the Act were altered; more social adequacy was built into the system, even though the "proportionality principle" continued. Benefit payments for low-income groups and those already nearing retirement age were increased by revision of the benefit formula. The financial management of the reserve fund that had come under considerable criticism was also liberalized. [25]

In the area of unemployment insurance, the 1939 amendments modified the definition of "covered employment" and made the tax

applicable only to the first $3,000 in wages. There were also changes made in the assistance programs, such as the increase in the federal share of the costs. Annual authorization for grants for maternal and child health, crippled children's and child welfare services was increased. The changes instituted in the assistance programs, however, were not as far-reaching as those in the insurance programs. The principle of confidentiality of records was introduced together with the provision of appeals systems for those who were denied assistance. In regard to unemployment insurance and public assistance, the state personnel merit system was made a prerequisite for the approval of a state plan by the Social Security Board. It was also made a condition for federal grants for maternal and child health and crippled children's services. [26]

The amendments of 1939 were the first major revision in the provisions of the Social Security Act of 1935. This was only the beginning of a continuing process of extending coverage and increasing benefits, with a view to making the program more comprehensive and effective in the goal of meeting the real needs of millions of people.

The Aftermath of World War II and the 1946 Amendments

During the war years, there was no significant amendment to the Social Security Act; social legislation and domestic issues in general received a lower priority. Social Security became almost a dead issue as against the high priority for mobilizing the energies of the nation to win the war.

The need for changes in the Social Security program, nevertheless, were very real. The limitations of the 1939 amendments were becoming more evident. It has been argued that on the eve of World War II several improvements had to be made if Social Security were to signify anything more than an "empty term." [27] But these changes had to await the reordering of national priorities following the war.

While there was no important amendment to the Social Security

Act in the war years, there were some developments and proposals of significance. The President, in his periodic messages to Congress, and the Social Security Board, through its annual reports, continued to indicate the need for changes in Social Security legislation. In addition, the publication of the Beveridge Report in Britain and the Report of the National Resources Planning Board in the U.S. had some impact on the movement for liberalization of the social insurance program.

The Beveridge Report, submitted by Sir William Beveridge on November 20, 1942, recommended a comprehensive social insurance program for Britain after the war. Sir William was Chairman of Britain's Interdepartmental Committee on Social Insurance and Allied Services. His report was the result of the Committee's undertaking to survey existing social insurance and allied services and to recommend changes. The Committee in proceeding to make recommendations on social insurance identified three guiding principles which, in a sense, have significance for social insurance programs not only in Britain, but also in other parts of the world. Those guiding principles follow:

> The first principle is that any proposals for the future, while they should use to the full the experience gathered in the past, should not be restricted by consideration of sectional interests established in the obtaining of that experience. . . .
>
> The second principle is that organization of social insurance should be treated as one part only of a comprehensive policy of social progress. Social insurance fully developed may provide income security; it is an attack upon Want. But Want is one only of five giants on the road of reconstruction and in some ways the easiest to attack. The others are Disease, Ignorance, Squalor, Idleness.
>
> The third principle is that social security must be achieved by cooperation between the State and the individual. The State should offer security for service and contribution. The State in organizing security should not stifle incentive, opportunity, responsibility; in establishing a national minimum, it should leave

room and encouragement for voluntary action by each individual to provide more than that minimum for himself and his family. [28]

Apart from these guiding principles, it is interesting to note in passing that the scheme of social insurance suggested by the Committee embodied six basic principles: flat rate of subsistence benefit, flat rate of contribution, adequacy of benefit, comprehensiveness, classification, and unification of administrative responsibility. [29]

The exact influence of the Beveridge plan on the social insurance scene in the U.S. is hard to assess. It undoubtedly had a significant effect on the thinking of persons in the social insurance and social welfare fields. Policy makers, especially some of the congressional leaders, were aware of the scheme and its significance in the British context and outside. The arrival of Sir William on a lecture tour to the U.S., and his meeting congressional leaders informally to discuss his plan also stimulated further thinking and discussion. Altmeyer points out that President Roosevelt's reaction was somewhat mixed. The President did not, as might have been expected, capitalize on the Beveridge Report "as an occasion to dramatize the immediate need for sweeping congressional action." Needless to say this was partly due to his preoccupation with the war and the fact that the Democratic strength in Congress was weakened. [30]

The National Resources Planning Board's technical report, "Security, Work and Policies," was submitted to President Roosevelt on December 4, 1941, a few days prior to the United States' entry into World War II. It was essentially the work of the Technical Committee on Long-Range Work and Relief Policies, and was a significant effort to define the problem of public aid and to determine the objectives of programs. The Chairman of the Committee was William Haber. The members of the Committee were related either directly or indirectly to social welfare, labor and allied fields, and brought to bear their interests and concerns, including that of extending social insurance. Dr. Eveline Burns, in her capacity as Director of Research, played a crucial role in the Committee. [31]

The report, in outlining specific objectives of public aid policy, emphasized policies aiming at prevention of economic insecurity "through a fuller utilization" of the nation's "productive resource," including labor. It also made specific reference to the need for "assurance of basic minimum security through social insurance, so far as possible." There was also a new policy approach suggested—of viewing social stability as a function of economic security. [32] The National Resources Planning Board had hoped that its report would be looked upon as "the American Beveridge Plan." Even though the report had been submitted to the President on December 4, 1941, ahead of the publication of the Beveridge Report, President Roosevelt transmitted the National Resources Planning Board report to Congress only on March 10, 1943. [33] While there was no immediate congressional action, the recommendations embodied in that report were bound to be considered, even though not adopted *in toto,* in subsequent proposals for policy changes and amendment.

Social Security legislation had to await the end of the war, when there would be greater focus on the domestic scene and when the President's official support would be forthcoming. The war in Europe ended on May 8, 1945, and following this there were to be changes in Social Security, though limited, by way of amendments to the Act introduced in August 1946. These changes, however, were to occur under the administration of President Harry S. Truman, since President Roosevelt, the master builder who had laid the "corner stone" of the Social Security program in 1935 and who had guided the changes of 1939, had died on April 12, 1945.

President Truman, on the occasion of the tenth anniversary of the signing of the Social Security Act—August 14, 1945—issued a statement which seemed to indicate his commitment in broad terms to the policies pursued by Roosevelt in relation to Social Security changes. In the course of his statement he emphasized:

> ... We should lose no time in making of our Social Security Act a more perfect instrument for the maintenance of economic security throughout this country.

I expect to present to the Congress specific recommendations
toward this objective.
....True social security must consist of rights which are
earned rights—guaranteed by the law of the land. [34]

Despite the determination to carry forward his plans for liberalization of Social Security, Truman faced serious obstacles. He had
the difficult task of conducting business with a conservative post-war
Congress—particularly, the House of Representatives and its influential Ways and Means Committee. The President also did not have,
especially in the initial stages, the kind of prestige that his predeces-
sor had commanded. Truman's popularity in 1946 reportedly fell as
low as 32 percent. [35] It was in this atmosphere that any Social
Security policy changes and amendments had to be attempted.

Social reform movements and reformers, however, had continued
to urge the need for further amendments to make the promise of
social security a reality to several very large groups that were still
excluded. Abraham Epstein, through the medium of the National
Conference on Social Security and his talks and writings elsewhere,
persisted in pointing to the existing limitations, and the need for
further changes in Social Security. Epstein's death in 1942 removed
from the scene a dedicated, though difficult and uncompromising
champion, for the extension and liberalization of the program. The
American Federation of Labor had as early as 1940 made specific
recommendations to the platform and resolutions committee of
both parties for extension of Social Security. It had urged the
adoption of planks ensuring extension of coverage of old-age insurance, more inclusive coverage and more adequate unemployment
compensation benefits, permanent disability insurance and health
insurance. [36] Likewise the National Consumers' League had urged
both the Democratic and Republican parties in 1940 to adopt Social
Security planks in their platforms, ensuring extension of old-age
insurance, extending benefits of unemployment compensation to
groups not covered hitherto, and providing for a Federal system of
permanent disability insurance and health insurance. [37] Arthur

Altmeyer, still Chairman of the Social Security Board, addressing the National Conference of Social Work in 1943 on "Needed Changes and Expansion on Social Security," emphasized the introduction of a single comprehensive Federal system of contributory social insurance as the major policy change desirable. [38]

Representatives of the several reform movements also appeared before the House Ways and Means Committee 1946 hearings on Social Security legislation, from February 25 to June 7, to present their views. These hearings were held just a few months before the Social Security amendments were finally passed.

Despite the recommendations of the Social Security Board and the varying pressure exerted by reform movements for a more comprehensive Social Security program, there were no major alterations embodied in the amendments to the Act, adopted on August 10, 1946. The few innovations included changes in old-age and survivors' insurance. The Act was amended to provide monthly benefits under old-age and survivors' insurance of certain veterans of World War II. This was intended to close the gap in protection for families of veterans in the event of their deaths between the time of discharge from service and the date by which they were expected to acquire or re-establish protection through civilian employment. Survivors of qualified veterans who became beneficiaries under the Act were widows aged 65 and over, young dependent children, widows of any age with young dependent children, and aged dependent parents of the insured veteran who left no widow or child under 18.

Coverage of private maritime employment under state unemployment insurance was instituted, and temporary unemployment benefits were extended to seamen with wartime federal employment. Permission was granted for states with employee contributions under their unemployment insurance laws to utilize such funds for temporary-disability insurance benefits. Provision was also made for greater federal sharing in public assistance payments for a specified period. Increased grants were also made available for maternal and child health and child welfare services. [39]

The 1946 amendments left untouched the major issues of old-age

and survivors' insurance, such as extending coverage to farm workers, domestic workers and employees of nonprofit organizations, and increasing benefits rates. The whole issue of disability insurance also remained an open question with no policy decision. The changes introduced in 1946 were disappointing, especially in the context of the urgency felt immediately after the war, the representations made by the reform movements, the recommendations in the National Resources Planning Board Report, and President Truman's intent as expressed in periodic messages to Congress.

The Amendments of 1950 and 1952

The 1950 amendments to the Social Security Act were the first major revision since 1939. Seldom, it is pointed out, did such a single piece of legislation receive "such long and intensive consideration." They were the result of a long series of investigations and reports, spread over ten years. The Advisory Council on Social Security of 1948 had emphasized the need for changes, pointing to serious shortcomings, such as restricted coverage, inadequate benefits and stringent eligibility requirements.

Though, in a sense, sentiment was favorable to changes in Social Security following World War II, the amendments of 1950 did not come easily. In 1948, Congress had avoided action on President Truman's recommendations and the recommendations of the advisory Council on Social Security. Instead Congress, which was predominantly Republican, passed two bills which excluded newspaper and magazine vendors from the coverage that they already had, and narrowed the definition of "employee" in the Social Security Act. [40]

President Truman made this legislative action of the Republican Congress—reducing coverage in social insurance—a major issue in the 1948 presidential campaign. Another issue that emerged was the introduction of a national health insurance program. The President's re-election and a Democratic Congress gave the impetus and was deemed a mandate for progressive Social Security changes. It should

be noted, however, that following World War II, the very continuation of the old-age and survivors' insurance system as "a contributory wage-related system," remained a critical question and a basic policy issue. [41]

The Social Security Act amendments of 1950, approved on August 28, resulted in significant policy changes in the Social Security programs. This was particularly true of the old-age and survivors' insurance program where there were substantial enlargements of the coverage, benefits and eligibility provisions. The 1950 amendments introduced the first large-scale extension of old-age and survivors' insurance coverage since the passage of the Social Security Act in 1935. About 10,000,000 additional workers were covered, which included the self-employed, regularly employed farm and domestic workers, outside salesmen, federal civilian employees and certain categories of Americans employed abroad. [42] Of these over 7½ million workers were covered on a compulsory basis and about 2½ million on an optional basis. [43] The largest group among those newly covered were the nonfarm self-employed persons. The hitherto grave injustice, in the denial of protection to small businessmen, even though they were compelled to contribute to the protection of their employees, was corrected. The extension of compulsory coverage was achieved by including occupations previously excluded, broadening the definition of the term "employee" and by extending coverage to new geographical areas—Puerto Rico and the Virgin Islands. The new device of voluntary coverage affected two groups, employees of state and local governments and employees of nonprofit organizations. Employees of state and local governments, not already covered by a retirement system, were to be covered if their state made an agreement to that effect with the federal government. Employees of nonprofit organizations were to be covered, if their employer were agreeable and if two-thirds of the employees were in favor of coverage. [44]

The benefit payments were greatly liberalized under the 1950 amendments—benefits being increased by about 80 percent on the average. The increase in benefits, though they fell short of what was

recommended, at least corrected the inequity that was there, in that the original benefits had not been brought into line with the increase in price levels. Under a new formula introduced for computing benefits, the average benefits on retirement, hitherto $26 per month, were increased to $45 per month. In the event of an insured worker's dying prior to or after his retirement, his dependents were entitled to survivors' benefits which were almost doubled under the 1950 amendments. The maximum benefits payable to all members of a family was increased from $85 to $150 per month. [45]

The amendments of 1950 liberalized considerably the eligibility requirements for benefits under old-age and survivors' insurance. The changes introduced corrected the restrictive conditions which were added to the original Act by the amendments of 1939. Following enactment of the 1950 amendments, many persons, covered for tax purposes but ineligible for benefits hitherto, became eligible. The "new start" in eligibility requirements resulted in immediate benefit payments to many persons aged 65 and over who had not met the requirements of the earlier law. This sweeping change in eligibility requirements, as well as the substantial increases in benefits and expanded coverage, were approved by Congress in the hope of eliminating the need for further expansion in public assistance. There was also an increase in federal grants for maternal and child welfare, and a new federally aided assistance program—aid to permanent and totally disabled—was created.

The 1950 amendments, though they represent a major advance in the Social Security programs, fell short of the recommendations made by President Truman and the Administration. The extension of coverage under old-age and survivors' insurance did not include, for example, the farm operators. Professional persons were not included in the category of self-employed persons who were given coverage. Perhaps the most serious omission was the lack of provision for permanent and temporary disability insurance. This was provided for in the bill that was passed initially by the House but was deleted in the Senate. Opposition to the provision of disability insurance benefits came from the American Medical Association,

certain employers' organizations and casualty insurance companies, chiefly on the basis of administrative difficulties and increased costs. The representatives of the American Medical Association testified that

> to initiate a Federal disability program would represent another step toward wholesale nationalization of medical care and the socialization of the practice of medicine. [46]

Despite these limitations the Amending Act of 1950, like the Amending Act of 1939, is to be viewed "as one of the major milestones in America's long road toward a satisfactory and acceptable social security system." [47] There were significant policy changes in the extension of coverage to certain employments hitherto excluded, such as agriculture, domestic service and self-employment, in the substantial liberalization of benefit payments, and in the sweeping revision in eligibility requirements. The Amending Act also went a long way toward answering the basic Social Security policy issue of the time—whether "the typical form of publicly assured income" was to be social insurance or public assistance. [48] The amendments affirmed the intention of making the social insurance device the main form of public social security provision towards old-age and the death of the breadwinner. The changes also evidenced an emphasis on the "social" aspects of insurance and a movement away from the concept of private insurance. This was reflected in such new provisions as higher minimum benefits, the availability of benefits to persons with short periods of covered employment, and the heavy weighting of the first hundred dollars in the benefit formula. [49]

The provisions of the Amending Act of 1950 represent a compromise, a determined effort to reconcile differing and, in some instances, opposing points of view. Some provisions of the Act can be explained only in terms of the effort by Congress to accommodate, insofar as possible, the conflicting views and interests of numerous special groups. [50] This was perhaps most evident in the unique

provision regarding the coverage of employees of most nonprofit organizations, made available on a voluntary basis under certain specified conditions. Clergymen and members of religious orders, however, were excepted. Subsequent amendments were to make further changes in these provisions on the basis of changing conditions, new needs and demands.

President Truman in his State of the Union Message and his Budget Message in 1951 referred to the need for further improvements in the Social Security program and took the opportunity to reaffirm the policy direction reflected in the 1950 amendments—that social insurance rather than public assistance would be the "primary vehicle for providing social security." Again, in January 1952, the President in his messages to Congress emphasized the need for extension and liberalization of the Social Security system. Among the recommendations made were further extension of coverage, more liberal retirement and survivors' benefits, provisions for permanent and total disability insurance, and the strengthening of the federal-state unemployment insurance system. [51]

The Social Security Act amendments of 1952 were introduced as H.R. 7800 in Congress on May 12, 1952, approved by both Houses of Congress on July 16, and were signed into law on July 18 by President Truman. The enactment of this legislation within such a short time was unprecedented in the history of Social Security legislation since 1935. [52] Apart from President Truman's interest in expanding Social Security legislation and the continuing demand by various reform movements for improvement, there were special circumstances that seemed to help in the passage of the bill, despite the attempts made to postpone and to prevent its enactment. First, the absence of any major tax bill before Congress in 1952 meant that the House Ways and Means Committee was in a position to devote more time than ordinarily to Social Security legislation. Second, the keen interest and the prestige of Chairman Robert L. Doughton of the House Ways and Means Committee was a favorable factor. He was due to retire from Congress at the end of the session and several majority members of the Committee, recognizing the

fact that he was the sponsor of the original Act of 1935 and the amendments of 1939, felt that there should be a final piece of legislation in 1952 bearing his name, effecting further improvements in the Social Security program. Third, the general increase in prices and wages made possible the financing of benefit increases without any increase in the insurance contribution rate. The House Committee on Ways and Means in its report indicated that the major reason for the legislation was the rapid increase in wages and prices, which made immediate benefit adjustments imperative. [53]

The 1952 amendments, however, failed to carry forward the movement towards extension of coverage and increased benefits in any significant way. The increase in benefits under old-age and survivors' insurance barely kept pace with increases in price and wage levels and there was no extension of coverage. Besides the increase in benefits, other changes included the liberalization of the retirement test, the extension of the period of wage credits for military service through December 31, 1953, and the liberalization of the grant formula for public assistance payments. Perhaps the only significant change, especially from a long-term point of view, was the somewhat "inconclusive" legislative effort designed to preserve the rights of the permanent and totally disabled. It was important in that it opened up the problem of providing for permanent and total disability; a larger number within Congress and outside became concerned and, though action was stifled, it no longer could be postponed.

This attempt to provide for the insurance rights of the disabled in the 1952 law is a unique arrangement in the history of federal legislation. Section 3 of the 1952 law provided for the preserving of the insurance rights of the disabled and Section 216 (i) (2) stated that no application could be filed prior to July 1, 1953. But Section 221 stated that the law would cease to be in effect at the close of June 30, 1953. In short, the law providing for the preservation of the insurance rights of the permanent and totally disabled was to be automatically repealed the day before it went into operation. [54]

This was largely due to the attempt by Congress, in the face of

opposition by the American Medical Association to the disability freeze provisions, to comply with the persistent demands of Congressman Doughton, Chairman of the House Ways and Means Committee, that provision for preservation of the insurance rights of the disabled be in the law. Chairman Doughton's insistence, his prestige, and his forthcoming retirement from Congress at the end of the session were the deciding factors in the inclusion of the disability rights provision, though in an "inconclusive" almost abortive form in the law. [55]

The 1952 amendments, though they did not increase benefits or extend in coverage, were unique in other respects. The fact that legislation provided for increases in Social Security payments twice within two years was unprecedented, and indicated national awareness of the necessity and the possibility of altering programs to align with economic development. It is perhaps even more meaningful that the changes providing for increase in benefits were the result of a compromise agreement by both parties. Indeed, several members of both parties publicly declared that the increase was inadequate and that it should be more substantial. [56]

The Significance of the 1954 Amendments

The fundamental policy question—whether old-age insurance should be contributory and wage-related or take the form of a flat pension financed from general revenue—continued to be debated throughout the 1935-1954 period. In a sense the amendments of 1950 had given a clear indication of policy direction, of continuing the contributory wage-related system. But there were to be further challenges to this decision and attempts made to change the direction of policy, notably by the Chamber of Commerce and Congressman Carl Curtis, Chairman of the House Sub-committee on Social Security. The special significance of the amendments of 1954 is in the decisive upholding of the contributory wage-related insurance system, in the face of strong pressures to introduce some form of uniform scheme that might embody low benefit rates.

President Eisenhower, shortly after his inauguration, in his State of the Union Message of February 2, 1953, recommended that the "old-age and survivors' insurance laws should promptly be extended to cover millions of citizens who have been left out of the social security system." However, he did not give any indication as to what his stand was in regard to the proposals of the U.S. Chamber of Commerce, which seemed to threaten the existing contributory wage-related old-age insurance system. The Board of Directors of the Chamber of Commerce had, on November 15, 1952, a few days after the election of a Republican President, made this policy declaration on Social Security:

Experience now demonstrates that adherence to the basic purpose of a sound social security program for the aged requires:

(a) Adoption of a reasonable plan in lieu of federal grants for old-age assistance, to extend immediate protection under the old-age and survivors' insurance system to the present unprotected aged; and

(b) Periodic adjustment of the equal taxes on employer and employees and the tax on self-employed to support benefit disbursements on a current basis. [57]

The policy hinted at here was that of a uniform pension scheme, on a pay-as-you-go basis, to be made available to all aged irrespective of contributions, with the possibility of the benefit rate's being lower than before.

Following Eisenhower's State of the Union Message, Mrs. Oveta Culp Hobby, the Federal Security Administrator who later became Secretary of the newly constituted Department of Health, Education and Welfare, named an advisory group on Social Security to explore various alternatives for extending Old-Age and Survivors' Insurance coverage. There were five persons appointed as members of this advisory group, the majority of whom were spokesmen for the policies advocated by the Chamber of Commerce. There were no

representatives of organized labor, farm organizations or other groups advocating improvements in Social Security. The only exception was the appointment of Dr. Eveline Burns, Professor, New York School of Social Work, who had close relations with a number of reform movements.

The predominance of Chamber of Commerce spokesmen in this advisory group raised fears and protests that they were in a position to virtually dictate Social Security policies. The role of some of the reform movements, particularly labor, in ensuring that some of their representatives have a voice in this influential advisory group was consequential. Editorials and news items in labor publications raised a hue and cry that although several of the appointed "advisors" had denounced Social Security as "Fabian Socialism" leading to "tyranny and dictatorship," the government was seeking their "advice" on how to improve the Social Security program. The American Federation of Labor *News Reporter,* commented cynically that it was "like appointing professional arsonists to handle arrangements for National Fire Prevention Week." [58]

Mrs. Hobby responded immediately to this unfavorable publicity by appointing seven additional members to the advisory group; Dr. Eveline Burns was now joined by other respresentatives of reform movements, such as Nelson Cruikshank, Director of Social Insurance Activities, American Federation of Labor; Katherine Ellickson, Secretary, Social Security Committee, Congress of Industrial Organizations; and Loula Dunn, Director, American Public Welfare Association. The advisory group, however, was still dominated numerically by representatives of the Chamber of Commerce, insurance companies and other groups not likely to favor moves towards liberalization of Social Security programs. Indeed some of the insurance companies viewed the existing program as "creeping socialism."

There were other developments such as the social security conference sponsored by the U.S. Chamber of Commerce held in Chicago on March 27, 1953, where the Chamber launched a nationwide "grassroots" campaign for sweeping revisions in the Social Security system. The proposals put forward there were cloaked in such

appealing terms as "broadened coverage" and "pay-as-you-go," while actually they suggested regressive changes which posed serious threats to the social security program. [59] One of the speakers at this conference was Congressman Carl T. Curtis, chairman of the Subcommittee on Social Security of the House Ways and Means Committee, who in a minority report submitted in 1949 had referred to the Social Security system as "totally unmoral."

As Chairman of the House Subcommittee on Social Security, Congressman Curtis was entrusted with the task of conducting studies and investigations on all matters pertaining to Social Security laws. He had also been invited to participate in the deliberations of the advisory group on Social Security. It should be noted that Arthur Altmeyer, who had achieved a distinct leadership role in the development of the Social Security program from its inception, was not invited to meet with this advisory group. Indeed a short time after the advisory group began to hold its meetings, on April 10, 1953 Altmeyer ceased to be Commissioner of Social Security.

It was apparent that forces opposed to substantial changes and improvements in the contributory social insurance system were gaining control. The very principle of contributory social insurance seemed to be in jeopardy. The reform movements, labor particularly, continued to voice alarm at attacks on Social Security. The Congress of Industrial Organizations, in a telegram sent to Mrs. Hobby on May 6, 1953, lashed out at "wolf-in-sheep-clothing" proposals which would endanger the program. [60] Joseph Curran, Chairman of the CIO Social Security Committee, made public the telegram urging, among other things, the appointment to the position of Commissioner a person committed to public service rather than front men for organizations hostile to social security. He urged Mrs. Hobby "to take courageous leadership" against the "insidious attacks upon the social security structure."

Alarmed at the threats to the Social Security program, representatives of reform movements and other civic and educational groups met at a Citizens Conference on Social Security in Washington, D.C. on May 14, 1953 "to launch a drive to protect and improve the

social security gains of the past eighteen years." The sponsors of the conference included Miss Elizabeth Magee of the National Consumers' League (co-chairman), Mrs. Marie Lane of the American Public Welfare Association, Mrs. Katherine Ellickson of the Congress of Industrial Organizations, and Mr. Nelson Cruikshank of the American Federation of Labor. The sponsors declared that there was a "crisis" confronting the Social Security program, that the time-tested program was "in danger of being destroyed by ill-considered proposals for its complete overhauling. [61]

Special concern was expressed about the proposals made to change the program, with a view to blanketing in 5,000,000 aged persons not eligible to Social Security benefits by charging them against the existent reserve fund rather than providing more satisfactory arrangements. Such a plan, it was argued, would shift the burden of providing the required funds from "the general taxpayer, on whom are levied progressive income taxes based on ability to pay, to workers and employers through regressive payroll taxes." The citizens conference urged the provision of adequate aid to the 5,000,000 aged, but pointed out that the proposal to finance this aid through the 18 billion dollar reserve fund would undermine the existent fund. Serious objections were also raised regarding the plan of paying the 5,000,000 aged persons, not covered by the Social Security program, a low sum of $25 a month.

The Citizens Conference on Social Security was timely and spoke out on issues that were vital. Even though the exact influence it exerted on policy makers is hard to assess, it was at least clear evidence of dismay by a representative group at the attempts to reverse Social Security policies and to hold back improvements in programs. This mobilization of forces in favor of progressive reform in Social Security and the indication of concern were vital, especially in the context of the regressive measures suggested by the earlier conference sponsored by the U.S. Chamber of Commerce.

It is interesting to note the diverse responses that this Citizens Conference on Social Security evoked. Arthur Altmeyer, even though he was not able to participate due to prior commitments,

responded favorably to the idea of having such a conference. "I feel strongly," wrote Altmeyer, "the necessity for greater citizen participation." This he indicated was necessary not only for preserving the progress already made, but also in going forward, "toward our goal of achieving greater social security for the American people." In his moving letter written to the chairman of the Conference, a month after he had ceased to be Commissioner of Social Security, Altmeyer went on to say:

> In a world so torn by suspicion, strife and bloodshed, social security offers some continuing assurance of our common humanity, representing as it does a great cooperative effort to protect ourselves and our fellow citizens against the great economic hazards that spell want and suffering even in a land of plenty.
> The quest for social security is an ancient quest and a never ending quest. It is by no means a frill or a social worker's dream or a demagogue's delight. Those who say that the people cannot have both liberty and security do not understand the meaning of these concepts. In our democracy the positive idea of liberty in the sense of true equality of opportunity must prevail. . . . [62]

In obvious contrast to Altmeyer's response to the idea of a citizens conference and the views expressed in his letter was the news release issued by the U.S. Chamber of Commerce, declaring that businessmen of America were shocked by the unprincipled attacks made on their "non-discriminatory social security program" at what it termed "a conference of self-appointed planners of American family life." Amusingly in retrospect, the Chamber then went on to raise the cry of communist influence. "The so-called citizens conference on social security," said the news release, "included several principals who have been cited in Government publications for involvement in communist front activities." [63]

The National Conference of Social Work annual meeting, opening on May 31, 1953, also provided a forum for the discussion of the ·Curtis–Chamber of Commerce approach to Social Security versus that espoused by the previous Administration and progressive

groups. Congressman Curtis addressed the social work conference on the opening night and posed a challenge to the old-age and survivors' insurance system as it had developed. The next day Dr. Altmeyer at the conference was called upon to give his reactions to Curtis's views and proposals. It should be noted that Curtis's rhetoric was such that the real issues seemed to be unclear. It was hard to disagree with him, and he seemed to ask the right questions. Altmeyer in the course of his remarks indicated the misstatements in Congressman Curtis's speech and gave reasons to justify the claim that contributory social insurance was the device best suited to attain the "twin goals of social adequacy and individual liberty."

Altmeyer also urged the Conference to develop and support proposals designed to improve the existing OASI system in these specific ways:

1. Extend coverage to include all gainfully occupied persons.
2. Increase the maximum income which serves as the basis for contributions and benefits.
3. Restore the 1% increment in benefit amount for each year of contribution.
4. Reduce the qualifying age for women's retirement benefits to 60 years.
5. Provide for a more adequate benefit formula in compensating for loss of income.
6. Pay the same benefits for retirement due to permanent total disability as are paid for old-age retirement. [64]

The election of Arthur J. Altmeyer as President of the National Conference of Social Work for 1954-1955 clearly indicated which approach to social insurance social workers favored.

It should be noted that, despite the attacks on the Social Security system by Congressman Curtis, the Chamber of Commerce and others, President Eisenhower seemed intent on fulfilling his campaign pledges. His demand for immediate action to extend Social Security coverage was sufficient evidence of this, but he was looking for responses from interested and influential groups to justify action.

The opposition of the labor movement was perhaps the most important factor in deterring the Administration's endorsement of the plan presented by the Chamber of Commerce. [65] But the role of other movements and individual reformers, such as Altmeyer, Witte and Burns, was also significant.

The consultants on Social Security appointed to study the program submitted their report to Secretary Oveta Hobby on June 24, 1953, recommending coverage of nearly 10,500,000 more persons. The consultants pointed out that, while they had confined their study as requested to extension of coverage, it was not possible in actual practice to separate the different aspects of social insurance such as coverage, benefits and financing. They recommended extension of coverage to about 6,500,000 additional persons on a compulsory basis, including self-employed farm operators, certain categories of farm workers hitherto uncovered and self-employed professional persons excluded by the 1950 amendments. In addition they recommended coverage on a voluntary basis to about 4,000,000 state and local employees, as well as to ministers and members of religious orders. Reacting to the controversy over the blanketing-in of persons already 65 or over, not eligible for coverage under the existing program, the consultant group declared:

... our recommendations for extension of coverage at this time do not include the blanketing-in of persons already age 65 or over who because they have not become eligible through prior work in covered employment are not receiving insurance benefits. We have excluded this group from consideration in this report because their inclusion would involve very substantial modifications of the present program which would require careful and prolonged study. [66]

On August 1, 1953, President Eisenhower submitted a special message to Congress transmitting the Social Security consultants' report, with the recommendation of the Secretary of the Department of Health, Education and Welfare, indicating the need to cover specific additional groups. Two days later, Representative Daniel

Reed, Chairman of the House Ways and Means Committee, introduced H.R. 6812 (by request) to implement the recommendations. Again on January 14, 1954, the President transmitted a special message to Congress, recommending changes in the old-age and survivors' insurance and public assistance programs. On the same day, H.R. 7199 and H.R. 7200 were introduced to implement the President's recommendations on old-age and survivors' insurance and public assistance respectively. The Ways and Means Committee held public hearings on H.R. 7199 from April 1 to 15.

Spokesmen for the various reform movements, especially labor, the Townsend Movement, the American Association for Social Security, the American Public Welfare Association and the American Association of Social Workers, testified before the Ways and Means Committee in behalf of H.R. 7199.

Testimony before Congressional committees was but one form of activity to influence policy changes in social insurance utilized by the reform movements. As in the case of the previous amendments, diverse methods were used but they had two main thrusts—educational work and lobbying. The American Association of Social Workers, with the help of Elizabeth Wickenden who served as consultant on Public Social Policy, stepped up its efforts and through the medium of its *Public Social Policy Bulletin* and other publications and its Committee on Public Social Policy, kept its members informed of legislative developments, issues and possible action to be undertaken. The *Public Social Policy Bulletin* numbers 1 and 2, for example, appearing in November 1953 and January 1954 respectively, were devoted entirely to social security issues and developments and included specific comments on the Administration bill, H.R. 7199, and other proposals. [67] They also had practical suggestions for action.

The Social Security Act amendments of 1954, approved on September 1, embodied provisions significant not only in their coverage of new groups, but also in ensuring the development of a progressive OASI program. The amendments extended old-age and survivors' insurance to farmers, self-employed members of specified

professions and additional farm and domestic employees; coverage was made available on a voluntary group basis to members of state and local government retirement systems; and, at their individual option, to ministers and members of religious orders. Decision was also made to raise to $4,200 the earnings base for tax and benefit computation purposes. There was an increase in ultimate contribution rates and in benefits. The retirement test was liberalized and allowance was made for a drop-out of four or five years of lowest earnings in computing benefits. Protection for the benefit rights of disabled persons was also made available through a disability-freeze provision, despite the opposition of the American Medical Association. [68] Nonetheless, in terms of strides still to be taken by way of insurance provisions for disability, it amounted to a mere token provision. However, with increased public interest and concern for the provision of disability insurance, it was clear that it could not be held back any longer. By 1956, disability insurance was to be added to the program.

The amendments of 1954 extended old-age and survivors' insurance coverage to a point where it was nearly universal. Approximately 9 out of every 10 gainfully employed persons were covered. With these new, hard-won gains the Social Security program now became a more effective force in preventing family insecurity and in contributing to socio-economic welfare. The coverage of farm operators and additional farm workers was of considerable import, not only in relation to the large number of persons newly covered, but also to the fact that, hitherto, farm people had no real opportunity to participate in any social insurance program. [69] Table 14 indicates the new groups to whom coverage was extended under the 1954 amendments and the approximate number of persons in each of them. As reported in Table 14, farm operators were the largest group covered under the 1954 amendments. An important consideration in extending coverage to a large number of farm families was the hope that this would help to curtail the growth of public assistance costs in rural areas. Indeed, an argument put forward by labor, the American Public Welfare Association and other reform

TABLE 14

PERSONS NEWLY COVERED BY OLD-AGE AND SURVIVORS' INSURANCE UNDER THE 1954 AMENDMENTS TO THE SOCIAL SECURITY ACT.

Covered Group	Estimated Number of Workers During a Year
TOTAL	9,950,000*
Farm operators	3,600,000
Farm workers	2,100,000
State and local government employees under retirement systems	3,500,000
Self-employed professionals	150,000
Ministers	250,000
Domestic workers	200,000
Federal civilian employees	150,000
Fishermen	50,000
Homeworkers	100,000
U.S. Citizens employed by foreign subsidiaries of American corporations	100,000
Employees whose service is not in the course of the employer's business (casual labor)	50,000

*Total is less than the sum of the separate coverage groups because an estimated 300,000 persons who will be covered both as hired farm workers are included in both groups.
Source: Social Security Bulletin, January 1955, p. 4. Table 1. See note 69.

movements for the extension of social insurance in general had been that it would help to reduce public assistance costs everywhere. It is noteworthy that in the early years of the Social Security program more aged persons received assistance payments than insurance benefits. However the situation changed and, by January 1955, aged persons receiving insurance benefits numbered 5.5 million, more than double the 2.5 million. The turning point had come after the 1950 amendments when requirements for insured status were liberalized and benefits increased substantially. [70]

Table 15 indicates the changes in the minimum and maximum benefit provisions under the amendments of 1954, in comparison with changes introduced by previous amendments since 1935.

As indicated in Table 15, the original Act (1935) provided only retirement benefits for the individual insured worker. Subsequent policy changes resulted in the amendments providing supplementary benefits for the dependents of a retired worker and for survivors of deceased workers as well. By 1954, the minimum old-age benefit had tripled while the increase in maximum old-age benefit was only about 28 percent. Undoubtedly this trend reflects greater focus on the interests of the lower-income worker.

An important policy issue, the concept of compulsory insurance, introduced in the original Act, though not reversed was subject to certain modifications in the amendments of 1954. Coverage on a group voluntary basis was extended to additional state and local government employees. Ministers and certain members of religious orders were to participate in the OASI program on the basis of individual election. It should be noted that, while proposals for coverage on an individual elective basis were made in regard to other groups such as farm operators and self-employed persons, Congress allowed coverage on this basis to only the clergy. In providing coverage for clergy on an individual basis in the 1954 amendments, the Committee on finance stated:

A provision for coverage on an individual election basis, while not generally desirable, is considered by your Committee to be

TABLE 15

MINIMUM AND MAXIMUM BENEFIT PROVISIONS UNDER THE SOCIAL SECURITY ACT AND ITS AMENDMENTS

(Monthly Amounts Except for Lump-sum Death Payments)

Item	Year of Legislation				
	1935	1939	1950	1952	1954
Minimum old-age benefit [a]	$10.00	$ 10.00	$ 20.00	$ 25.00	$ 30.00
Maximum old-age benefit [a]	85.00	[b] 60.00	80.00	85.00	108.50
Minimum family benefit [c]	[d]	10.00	15.00	18.80	30.00
Maximum family benefit [c] [e]	[d]	85.00	150.00	168.80	200.00
Minimum lump-sum death payment [f]	[g]	60.00	60.00	75.00	90.00
Maximum lump-sum death payment	[g]	[b] 360.00	240.00	255.00	255.00

[a] Payable to retired worker.
[b] Assumes that 50 years to coverage is the maximum possible.
[c] Total benefit payable to retired worker and dependents or to all survivor beneficiaries.
[d] No benefits provided for dependents or survivors.
[e] Maximum provision of 80 percent of average monthly wage also applicable but application may not reduce benefit to less than $25 for 1939 law, $40 for 1950 law, $45 for 1952 law, and $50 or 1½ times primary insurance amount for 1954 law. In some cases slightly larger amounts can be paid as the result of the provision for rounding benefit amounts (to next higher 10 cents for each beneficiary).
[f] Under the 1939 and later laws, the lump-sum payment is made to the surviving widow or widower who lives with the deceased person at time of death. When there is no such survivor, the lump-sum payment cannot exceed burial expenses.
[g] No minimum or maximum provided (potential maximum was about $5,000).
Source: Robert J. Meyers. "Old-Age and Survivors' Insurance: History of the Benefit Formula," *Social Security Bulletin*, May 1955, p. 14. Table 1.

justified in this area because of the special circumstances. Many churches have expressed the fear that their participation in the old-age and survivors' insurance program as employers of ministers might interfere with the well established principle of separation of church and state. Many church representatives also believe that individual ministers who do not wish to be covered on grounds of conscience should not be required to participate in the program. [71]

However, today the issue of separation of church and state and its desirability is increasingly being discussed in many circles, indicating the possibility that principles which were the basis of policy decisions at one time may be subject to review and modification subsequently, necessitating changes in policy.

The amendments of 1954 take their place with the "milestones of progress" in Social Security, marked by the passage of the Act itself, and the amendments of 1939 and 1950—even though they did leave behind "unfinished business." They gave a firm endorsement to the contributory wage-related principle on which the old-age insurance and survivors' insurance had been based in the face of serious threats posed by the Curtis—Chamber of Commerce proposals. Reflecting on the significance of the post-1954 amendments, Nelson Cruikshank, Director, Social Insurance Activities of the American Federation of Labor, wrote:

It has been a long, tortuous journey . . . It was a journey beset with frightening perils and pitfalls. . . . Time was not so long ago when the roar of a sub-committee Chairman like Congressman Curtis of Nebraska sounded like that of a hungry lion in the jungle. With appetite whetted by his $100,000 appropriation to "study" social security . . . he stalked to and fro over the face of the earth threatening a quick, though far from painless, death to the system which four years before he had characterized as "totally immoral."

It now seems hardly possible that only a few short months ago the U.S. Chamber of Commerce was able to quicken with fear the heartbeat of every adherent to the social security principles—not

to mention the millions of older people looking to the system for a degree of security. . . . [72]

Apart from the endorsement of the basic principles of social insurance that were challenged, the amendments of 1954 are also significant in that Social Security from then onwards ceased to be a partisan issue. The existing Social Security program was no longer identified with only the Democratic party. Though there were evidences of this in the manner in which the 1950 amendments were handled, from 1954 onwards it was pretty clear that both parties were committed to the contributory wage-related old-age insurance system. Social Security and social insurance were accepted as permanent, and became "a truly non-partisan feature" of the American way of life.

The amendments to the Social Security Act, up to 1954, introduced policy changes, such as extension of coverage to new groups, liberalization of benefit payments, provision for dependents and survivors, helping to move toward the goal of comprehensive social insurance for all. The 1935-1954 period, it is maintained, is consequential in that much of what happened during that time has provided the basis for future developments in social security. This does not however rule out the possibility of fundamental changes in the future. Arthur Altmeyer makes the comment that "social security will always be a goal, never a finished thing, because human aspirations are infinitely expansible—just as human nature is infinitely perfectible." [73]

It is in this context that any analysis of the policy issues and changes embraced by the original Social Security Act and its several amendments up to 1954—and, for that matter, subsequently—have to be viewed. In relation to the goal of universal, adequate and comprehensive coverage the policy decisions and changes reflected in the amendments to the original Act at the end of 1954 represent "unfinished business." The major gap in the social security provisions by the end of this period was the lack of provision for two forms of social insurance prevalent in the social security systems of

most developed countries—adequate insurance to cover disability and cost of medical care. Among the major groups still excluded from coverage under old-age and survivors' insurance at the end of 1954 were disabled workers, federal civilian employees if they were already covered under a retirement system, self-employed physicians, clergymen who did not elect to be covered and certain types of domestic and agricultural workers.

A number of basic policy questions to which policy makers associated with the various amendments to the Social Security Act had to address themselves during that period will continue to be raised. The question of how much economic security can a society afford is a recurring one. Are we fair to those whose wages are inadequate in terms of present family needs, but are nevertheless compelled to make contributory payments? Why are they compelled, but clergymen are given an option? How fast and how far can we move in extending Social Security benefits? Do we rule out the possibility of government contributions altogether? How much emphasis should be given to considerations of cost and the effect on business conditions in providing for Social Security? These are broad economic, social, political and philosophic questions which will continue to demand the attention of Social Security policy makers even in the future. [74] If the quest for Social Security is unending because "human aspirations are infinitely expansive," it is also important to recognize that Social Security is no panacea. Social Security does not satisfy all the economic needs of the individual, to say nothing about his even greater psychological, social and spiritual needs.

NOTES

1. Roosevelt's Comments upon Signing the Social Security Act, August 14, 1935. Altmeyer, *op. cit.*, p. 12.
2. Schottland, *op. cit.*, p. 38.
3. See Edwin E. Witte, "The Objectives of Social Security," in *Social Security Perspectives*. Robert J. Lampman, ed., Madison: The University of Wisconsin Press, 1962, pp. 101-107.
4. See Altmeyer, *op. cit.*, pp. 109-110.

5. Cohen, "Federalism and Social Insurance," Bowen et al., eds. *op. cit.*, p. 11.

6. Schottland, *op. cit.*, p. 186.

7. Cohen, *op. cit.*, p. 18.

8. Schottland, *op. cit.*, p. 48.

9. Note: John G. Winant was the first Chairman of the Social Security Board. Following his resignation on September 28, 1936, Arthur J. Altmeyer was appointed.

10. Rayback, *op. cit.*, p. 338.

11. Letter of President Franklin D. Roosevelt, April 28, 1938, File 011.1 Amendments 1938, *Records of the Chairman of the Social Security Board, 1935-1940;* National Archives, Record Group 47, Washington D.C. See also: Altmeyer, *op. cit.*, p. 91. Note: Altmeyer mentions that the President wrote this letter on his request. Even if this were the impetus for the President's letter, it still indicates his closeness to the program and his interest in liberalizing it.

12. Text of Governor Landon's Milwaukee Address on Economic Security, *The New York Times.* September 27, 1936, pp. 1-2.

13. Democratic National Campaign Committee Information Sheet, "The Truth About Social Security," Election Platform and Related Data, 1932-1936, *Arthur J. Altmeyer Papers,* Manuscripts Library, State Historical Society of Wisconsin.

14. Democratic National Platform. *Democratic and Republican Platforms, 1936.* West Virginia Blue Book, *op. cit.*, p. 679.

15. "Advisory Council on Social Security News Release, File Sen. 76 A−F 8 (129) Finance Social Security," *Records of the Legislative Division*, National Archives, Washington, D.C.

16. Lubove, *op. cit.*, p. 178.

17. Gaston V. Rimlinger, "American Social Security in a European Perspective," Bowen *et al., op. cit.*, p. 227.

18. Statement by Abraham Epstein, December 10, 1937. Legislation and Development—Social Security Act: Amendments proposed by unofficial groups, 1930's; *Edwin E. Witte Papers,* Manuscripts Library, State Historical Society of Wisconsin, pp. 1-3.

19. Altmeyer, *op. cit.*, p. 99.

20. U.S. Congress. House Committee on Ways and Means, *Social Security. Hearings Relative to the Social Security Act Amendments of 1939, 76th Congress, 1st session.* Washington, D.C.: U.S. Government Printing Office, 1939, Vol. 1, p. 598.

21. *Ibid.*, Vol. II, pp. 1006 and 1020.

22. *Ibid.*, pp. 1344-1345.

23. U.S. Congress, Committee on Ways and Means, *Social Security. Hearings Relative to the Social Security Act Amendments of 1939, 76th Congress, 1st Session.* Washington, D.C.: U.S. Government Printing Office, 1939, Vol. II, p. 1320.

24. Schottland, *op. cit.*, p. 69.

25. Hogan and Ianni, *op. cit.*, p. 504.

26. Altmeyer, *op. cit.*, pp. 278-279.

27. Hogan and Ianni, *op. cit.*, p. 505.

28. Sir William Beveridge. *Social Insurance and Allied* Services. New York: The Macmillan Company, 1942, pp. 6-7.

29. *Ibid.*, p. 9.

30. Altmeyer, *op. cit.*, p. 141.

31. Social Security Act, Changes in 1940's, Legislation and Development, *Edwin E. Witte Papers*, Manuscripts Library, State Historical Society of Wisconsin.

32. Hogan and Ianni, *op. cit.*, p. 511.

33. Altmeyer, *op. cit.*, p. 143.

34. President's Statement on the Tenth Anniversary of the Signing of the Security Act, President Truman's Speeches, Messages 1945-1953, *Arthur J. Altmeyer Papers*, Manuscripts Library, State Historical Society of Wisconsin.

35. Corning, *op. cit.*, p. 57.

36. American Federation of Labor Recommendation to the Republican National Committee, AFL December 1940, *Records of the Executive Director, Social Security Board 1935-1940*, National Archives, Record Group 47, Washington D.C.

37. National Consumers' League news release, July 10, 1940, Political Party Platform 1940-1944, 4 11-2, *National Consumers' League Papers*, Manuscript Division, Library of Congress, Washington D.C.

38. Arthur J. Altmeyer. "Needed Changes and Expansion of Social Security," Speeches by A. J. Altmeyer, *Records of the Bureau/Division of Research and Statistics 1946-1950*, National Archives, Record Group 47, Washington D.C.

39. Altmeyer, *op. cit.*, p. 280.

40. *Ibid.*, p. 163.

41. *Ibid.*, p. 169.

42. Rayback, *op. cit.*, p. 404.

43. For a fuller account, see: George J. Leibowitz. "Old-Age and Survivors' Insurance: Coverage Under the 1950 Amendments," *Social Security Bulletin.* December, 1950, pp. 1-9; see also Altmeyer, *op. cit.*, p. 185.

44. Eveline M. Burns. *The Social Security Act Amendments of 1950: An Appendix to the American Social Security System.* Boston: Houghton Mifflin, 1949, p. 450.

45. See Summary of principal provisions of the Social Security Act Amendments of 1950, File 011.1 October 1950, *Records of the Office of the Commissioner 1949-1950*, National Archives, Record Group 47, Washington D.C. See also Witte, *op. cit.*, pp. 161-166.

46. Altmeyer, *op. cit.*, pp. 185-186.

47. Burns, *op. cit.*, p. 473.

48. *Ibid.*, pp. 474-475.

49. *Ibid.*, p. 476.

50. *Ibid.*, p. 473.

51. Altmeyer, *op. cit.*, p. 193.

52. Wilbur J. Cohen. "The Legislative History of the Social Security Act Amendments of 1952," (unpublished report, Social Security Administration, Department of Health, Education and Welfare), Washington D.C., 1954, pp. 1-5.

53. See U.S. Congress. House, Committee on Ways and Means. *Social Security Act Amendments of 1952* (House Report 1944 on H. R. 7800, 82nd Congress; 2nd Session), Washington D.C.: U.S. Government Printing Office, 1952.

54. Cohen, *op. cit.*, p. 17.

55. *Ibid.*, p. 2.

56. *Ibid.*, pp. 10, 19 and 20.

57. Altmeyer, *op. cit.*, p. 206.

58. News extracts from *Labor*. March 28, 1953, Social Security Consultants' Early Materials 1952-1953, *Katherine Ellickson Collection*, Wayne State University Labor History and Urban Affairs Archives.

59. Democratic National Committee Research Division Fact Sheet 4/14/53, Social Security Amendments 1953, IV NN6, *National Consumers' League Papers*, Manuscripts Division, Library of Congress, Washington D.C.

60. CIO News Release 5/6/53, Social Security Consultants' Correspondence, 1953, 63-10, *Katherine Ellickson Collection*, Wayne State University Labor History and Urban Affairs Archives.

61. Citizens Conference on Social Security, News Release 5/13/53, Social Security Amendments 1953, Citizens Conference IV NN6, *National Consumers' League Papers*, Manuscripts Division, Library of Congress, Washington D.C.

62. Letter from Arthur Altmeyer to Phillip Schiff, May 9, 1953, regarding invitation to "Citizens Conference on Social Security," Social Security Amendments 1953 Citizens Conference, *NCLP, op. cit.*

63. U.S. Chamber of Commerce, News Release, May 15, 1953, regarding "Citizens Conference on Social Security," *ibid.*

64. Remarks of Arthur J. Altmeyer at Group Meeting 3—Public Issues in Social Welfare, National Conference of Social Work, June 1, 1953, Curtis Committee Hearings 1953, *Arthur J. Altmeyer Papers*, State Historical Society of Wisconsin. See also Altmeyer, *op. cit.*, pp. 221-223.

65. Altmeyer, *op. cit.*, p. 215.

66. Consultants on Social Security. A Report to the Secretary of Health, Education and Welfare on Extension of Old-Age and Survivors' Insurance to Additional Groups of Current Workers. Washington D.C.: U.S. Government Printing Office, 1954, p. 4.

67. See *Public Social Policy Bulletin*. AASW, No. 1, November 30, 1953, and No. 2, January 25, 1954.

68. Altmeyer, *op. cit.*, p. 283.

69. James E. Marquis. "Old-Age and Survivors' Insurance: Coverage under the 1954 Amendments," *Social Security Bulletin*. January 1955, pp. 3-4.

70. Victor Christagau. "Old-Age and Survivors' Insurance After Twenty Years," in Haber and Cohen, *Social Security: Programs, Problems, and Policies*. Illinois: Richard E. Irwin, Inc., 1960, p. 174.

71. U.S. Congress. Senate Committee on Finance, *Social Security Amendments of 1954*, Senate Report 1987 on H.R. 9366, 83rd Congress; 2nd Session, Washington, D.C., U.S. Government Printing Office, 1954, p. 9.

72. See Nelson H. Cruikshank. "The Social Security Amendments of 1954," *The American Federationist*, September 1954.

73. Schottland, *op. cit.*, p. 182.

74. *Ibid.*, p. 188.

IV

The Role of the Reform Movements in Influencing Policy Changes in Social Insurance

There was a time when social work was more or less synonymous with private charity. However, today's concept of social work is quite different. It recognizes that consideration of the needs of the individual inevitably requires consideration of the environmental forces which affect the well-being of the individual. That is to say, social work has extended its unique skills to the broader field of social policy, including the development and use of all resources—local, national, international—to promote the well-being of individuals and families generally.

> Arthur J. Altmeyer, Acceptance Speech at Presentation of Survey Award, June 1949.

The quest for social security is a part of our American tradition. It is as typically American as our desire for better housing, better education for our children and a fuller and more comfortable life. Success of democracy in the final analysis is measured by the extent that the basic human drive for self-realization is satisfied. Social security is essential to human welfare and happiness—the quest for it will be with us always.

> Harry Becker, Director UAW-CIO Social Security Department, August 1950.

REFERENCE has already been made in the previous chapter to the role of labor and other social reform movements in the effort to influence policy changes in social insurance in discussing the different amendments to the Act of 1935 and the process by which they became law. What is discussed here regarding the role of the respective reform movements in influencing policy changes is supplementary to what has already been said in examining the process by which policy changes emerged in the form of amendments to the Act in 1939, 1946, 1950, 1952 and 1954.

Organized labor's lack of interest in the initial stages of the economic security bill (1935) was noted earlier. It was only after the bill had passed the House and was reported out by the Senate Finance Committee that labor began to get seriously involved. It is pointed out that in the later stages of the bill, in the controversial Clark amendment and in the subsequent developments, labor did everything possible to ensure the passage of the bill. [1]

However, prior to the passage of the Social Security Act there was a time when labor looked upon proposals for Social Security with disfavor; it was felt that Social Security was something to bargain for in union negotiations with employers. Organized labor up to the 1930's viewed proposals for compulsory social insurance as a threat; it was interpreted as leading the way to the subordination of the labor movement to the state. Samuel Gompers' hostility to social insurance and his vowing to assist the forces opposed to compulsory social insurance was a serious obstacle to the social insurance movement. [2] Robert Bremner's comment that under the impact of the depression two barriers to the progress of the social insurance movement—"public indifference" and "hostility of organized labor"—broke down, is evidence of how removed and antago-

131

nistic organized labor was at one time to the cause of social insurance. [3]

Labor, which in Britain and Europe had been in the forefront of the movement, was in the United States opposed to proposals for social insurance up to the 1930's and became seriously involved only in the final stages of the passage of the Social Security bill of 1935 at which point, however, it gave all possible help to ensure its enactment.

From then on, organized labor played an increasingly active and effective role in working for passage of amendments to the Act, and in dealing with the policy issues and changes involved. The New Deal bestowed much needed power upon the unions through the National Labor Relations Act; and labor's progressive interest in Social Security policies and changes coincided with its increase in strength and power. Few would have predicted this possibility of a strong labor movement brought into being by the "spirit and promise of the New Deal." But as Richard Hofstadter has observed, by the end of 1937 it was clear that a necessary additional element had become an integral part of the "social base of reformism"—a powerful labor movement. [4]

However, the growing strength and power of the labor movement during the period from 1935 to 1954 should not be exaggerated. The two major union groupings in the labor movement, the AFL and CIO, were divided in the late 1930's and remained apart throughout the 1940's; formal merger occurred only in the latter part of the 1950's. But it is also evident that, despite these divisions, in regard to Social Security policies there was considerable cooperation and agreement between the AFL and CIO. While there were differences among leaders in the higher echelons of bureaucracy in both the AFL and CIO, at the middle level and around interests such as Social Security, effective collaboration did occur. The following extract from a letter by Nelson Cruikshank, Director, Social Insurance Activities of the AFL, commenting on Social Security objectives of the CIO and AFL gives evidence that there was basic common agreement:

... As a matter of fact, in the entire field of social security there have been only a few and relatively minor points of differences in positions. I might say that at times we have had differences in method, particularly in seeking legislative enactment, but on the whole we have been able to work amicably with the CIO on all major objectives. [5]

It should also be noted that the labor movement, despite its growing strength, was at times threatened by attacks on its prerogatives and had to face anti-labor sentiment. This was the case, for example, in the 1947 Congress when the Taft—Hartley law, introducing several restrictions on unions, was enacted. In such situations, obviously labor was preoccupied with fighting for its own interests and privileges. But for the most part, among the reform movements, organized labor became the primary driving force for policy changes in social insurance.

The varied devices utilized by the labor movement to influence policy changes in social insurance—press releases, letters to Congressmen, policy statements issued at national conventions, activity of members in Social Security advisory councils and special committees, and representation at Congressional hearings—have already been referred to in the previous chapter in relation to action for each of the amendments to the Act. From these it is evident that the part played by the labor movement during the 1935-1954 period was significant. By 1937 labor had begun to emerge as a strong spokesman for the movement for the extension of social insurance. Indeed, in June 1937 William Green, President of the American Federation of Labor, wrote to President Roosevelt urging him to appoint a Presidential Commission to study the working of the existing Social Security law, and to make recommendations. In this letter, Green stated:

The American Federation of Labor definitely feels that the provisions of the social security law should be steadily perfected in order to provide better against the eventualities of old-age and unemployment as well as to add provisions that will take care of

unemployment due to physical disabilities, both acute and chronic. To this end, may I urge upon you the desirability for the appointment of a Presidential Commission charged with studying experience under the present social security law and drafting measures to set up a satisfactory national plan for unemployment compensation with provisions for those disabled by disease. [6]

Writing the President directly, conveying important policy stands taken, and urging changes was one form of action undertaken by labor to affect policy. President Roosevelt's response to Green's letter, suggesting close cooperation of the Social Security Board with interested groups such as the AFL, was evidence of the influence that labor was already wielding:

. . . I agree with you that this is a subject which requires careful and sustained attention. However, I am inclined to think that it would be possible to make the greatest progress in the study of the complex questions involved, if the Social Security Board pursued the necessary studies and made the necessary contacts with the various interested groups, such as the American Federation of Labor, as its studies progressed.

I am therefore asking the Social Security Board to communicate directly with you to obtain such information as you have already collected and also to obtain your ideas as to ways and means of accomplishing the objectives desired. I am also asking the Social Security Board to maintain continued contact with you as its studies progress and to furnish me with a report from time to time of such progress. [7]

President Roosevelt, in suggesting that the Social Security Board and the American Federation of Labor keep in close touch with each other regarding Social Security issues and methods of accomplishing desired objectives, was endorsing a possible working relationship and a pattern that was to be of considerable value in the subsequent years in attempts to introduce progressive changes in Social Security.

The labor movement, working in close cooperation with the Social Security Board and other interest groups favoring progressive

social security measures, provided strong support for the social insurance policy changes in which it had a particular interest. Labor's role was especially significant when there were major attacks on the social insurance system. During the period from 1935 to 1954 there were two such attacks on the program to which reference has already been made. The first occurred in 1936 during the Presidential campaign, when the Republican candidate, Governor Landon, made a major bid for support by attacking the Social Security Act. The second attack on the contributory social insurance system, was made during 1953 and 1954, notably by the U.S. Chamber of Commerce and its ally, Congressman Carl Curtis. On both occasions and especially in the second—the Curtis–Chamber of Commerce attack on the Social Security program—organized labor came out strongly in support of the contributory wage-related OASI system.

But it should be noted that labor, too, was caught up in its day-to-day problems and that, in this sense, social reform was often a secondary consideration and not a life-and-death issue. [8] However, individual labor leaders (like Nelson Cruikshank and Katherine Ellickson, to whom we have referred frequently) in their efforts to broaden policy and to win Social Security improvements, undoubtedly reflected the zeal and the spirit of the social reformers.

The Townsend Movement

The Townsend Movement from its inception posed an alternative and a threat to the social insurance approach. The radical proposal of a flat pension of $200 per month for all aged persons, financed by a sales tax, had the enthusiastic endorsement of many aged Americans. While the Townsend Movement in no sense campaigned for the development of a progressive contributory social insurance program, the very threat of a radical alternative proposal, the support it seemed to command, and the pressure exerted by the movement in Congress and outside, contributed indirectly to policy changes, leading to extension and liberalization of social insurance programs. The

movement was successful in creating "a powerful political force." There were catch phrases and slogans, such as "$200 a month at 60" or "the abundant life begins here and now," which attracted millions of aged persons and sympathizers. The nature of the response which was evoked from the aged and the "inflated" claims of membership were such that they undoubtedly had some impact on the state legislatures, Congress and the President's office.

The growth of the movement in the early years was phenomenal. Less than two years after the initial Townsend club had been chartered (the plan was announced on January 1, 1934), it is reported that there were 7,000 clubs with a membership of over 1.5 million aged persons across the country. Several factors contributed to the appeal of the Townsend Plan to millions of Americans, especially the aged. The plan was simple and concrete; it represented a "radical-conservative synthesis"; it was not alien to the existing "socio-ideological climate"; it made a direct appeal to the aged; and, above all, it held out the promise of hope and optimism. [9]

The Social Security Act, and specifically its old-age insurance provisions, were to a large extent a response to the pressure exerted by the Townsend Movement. Undoubtedly there were other factors that influenced policy decisions, such as the depression of the 1930's, the leadership of President Roosevelt and his advisers, the agitation of other social reformers and movements; but the influence of the Townsend Movement and the economic panacea that it held out were of notable importance. Indeed, old-age insurance was not seriously considered for inclusion in the 1934 Wagner–Lewis bill, to which President Roosevelt gave support, and which focused only on unemployment insurance. It is evident that it was the pressure exerted by the Townsend Movement in 1934—an election year—that forced the inclusion of old-age insurance "as a political necessity."

The Townsend Movement helped to crystallize popular feeling in support of old-age security. Its impact on policy decisions and changes was not restricted to the Act of 1935. Even when each of the successive amendments to the Act was proposed, the Townsend-ites continued to exert pressure for more drastic legislation to

ensuring adequate old-age security. By the very threat of more extreme measures which they posed, they weakened the opposition of conservative elements to further liberalizations and extensions of Social Security.

However, in considering the extent of influence that the Townsend Movement exerted in policy changes in Social Security during the 1935-1954 period, it is important to recognize that, while the movement had a phenomenal growth in the first few years and mounted considerable pressure, by 1954 it was dwindling and ceased to be "a significant force in pension politics." Nevertheless, its influence upon the passage of the Social Security Act and its amendments in 1939 should not be minimized.

Its effect upon subsequent amendments, however, was less apparent, even though Townsend representatives continued to appear before Congressional hearings, and the Townsend national conventions, clubs, and newspaper continued to campaign for more adequate old-age security. It is to be remembered that the Townsend Movement developed within a socio-economic matrix characterized by sudden increase in the aged population, widespread unemployment, and the lack of adequate provisions for old-age security. [10] It was in a sense a "depression phenomenon," and with the subsequent improvements in the economic situation and alternate provisions for Social Security, radical proposals seemed to have a diminished appeal, even though indirectly they continued to exercise influence.

There were three identifiable phases in the "politics" in behalf of the Townsend Plan in Congress. In the first phase (1934-1935), the Townsend Plan was presented in its most radical form, but the organizers were ill-equipped for the "legislative battle."

During the second phase (1937-1939), there emerged a more experienced organization, capable of wielding considerable pressure, with a modified bill designed to be more attractive to Congress, but still advocating a radical plan of universal flat pensions. Such factors as the strong Democratic-Republican rivalry at the polls and the limitations of the existing Social Security provisions seemed to give

the Townsend Movement a favorable climate to push for their particular plan. Hence, the threat of their proposal was very real prior to the 1939 amendments, and helped indirectly to break the resistance of conservative elements who were opposing the reformers' efforts to carry the social insurance movement further and to ensure progressive policies. The third phase (from 1940 onwards) marked the considerable decline of Townsendite influence in Congress, inspite of their attempts to make their proposal more acceptable. [11]

The Townsend Plan, in its goal of giving the aged a central place in the American recovery program, appealed to the economic, emotional and deep psychological needs of the aged. Indeed, Dr. Townsend was hailed as a modern Messiah by his many supporters. Symbols, such as Townsend buttons, and special Townsend songs sung at convention, gave the aged people an opportunity to identify themselves publicly with the movement, ensuring their continuing support for it. [12] Songs, such as the following, sung at the Townsend meetings give further insights into the strategies used to rally support:

> We're going to town with the Townsend Plan
> We'll put new life in Uncle Sam
> We'll wipe the depression from the earth
> Our Nation is due for another birth
> We draw no lines of color or creed
> Of political parties we have no need
> We're on our way and we know where
> And we'll stir things up when we get there. . . .

> We're coming Fifty Million Strong
> The fight'll be hot and it won't be long
> If Congress bucks and won't behave
> We'll ride over them like a tidal wave
> When the battle smoke has blown away
> And our Country awakes to a better day
> The world will grasp us by the hand
> And thank the Lord for Townsend's Plan. [13]

It is interesting to note that the song makes the claim that the movement was "fifty million strong." The Townsendites reputedly exaggerated their membership figures very greatly. There is also evidence to indicate that they claimed signatories of their petitions to Congress as Townsend club members. It is estimated that in 1936 there were about 7,000 Townsend clubs, with a total membership of about 2 million. [14] Perhaps many aged persons believed that they were "fifty million strong" as they sang and it was intended to give them a psychological security, so vital for the the movement. They also seem to have been very self-sufficient in singing "of political parties we have no need." However, it raises the question whether they had any relationship with the Democratic and Republican parties and to what extent they made attempts to influence Social Security policies through those parties.

It is inconceivable that the Democratic Party, which played a major part in the introduction of the contributory old-age insurance system under the Social Security Act, could have had an ongoing working relationship with the Townsend Movement which advocated universal flat pensions. It has been pointed out that, "as the initial reform" establishing old-age pensions, it was the Social Security Act ushered in by the Democrats and not the Townsend Plan that set the "dominant pattern for the American Social Security System," and that the Democrats could not tolerate any threats to this program, above all from the Townsendites. It was also not possible for the Republican Party officially to adopt the Townsend Plan in place of the Social Security Act. But it should be noted that many Republicans "flirted with the Townsend Movement," because it seemed politically expedient to do so. [15] In such a situation the Townsendites undoubtedly would have made attempts to push for policy changes through this source, to gain acceptance for their flat pension idea. Ironically, such efforts contributed to further reforms and policy changes through the existing social insurance framework.

However, the potential and the danger that were present in such Republican–Townsend alliances to introduce drastic changes in Social Security should not be minimized. In 1938, for example,

success of a "Townsend-Republican Coalition" in Congressional elections and the agitation over old-age pensions nationwide seemed to open the way for Congressional consideration of the Townsend Plan and policies advocating universal flat pensions. More than ninety Republicans who had indicated some commitment to the Townsend Plan were elected to Congress in 1938, constituting over one-half of the Republican members in the House.

Edwin Witte, writing to Abraham Epstein in September 1938, commented that the Townsend Movement was politically stronger than ever. He expressed concern that politicians who cared more for office than for anything else were committing themselves to the Townsend bill or the General Welfare Federation bill or for both. He went on to say:

> Most of them hope that they never will be compelled to vote for the plan, but as the situation is developing the Townsendites will certainly have sufficient strength to bring on a vote in the next session of Congress. More and more it is becoming clear that the next major issue in relation to social security is whether we want the Townsend Plan or not. . . . the real issue is between the Social Security Act and the Townsend Plan. [16]

The dangers that this situation posed made further policy changes in Social Security imperative, leading to extension of coverage and liberalization of provisions. Policy changes introduced in the amendments of 1939, while basically aiming at strengthening the existing program to make it more responsive to the needs of people, were also a means to stem the tide of Republicans and Townsendites who became strange bedfellows seeking to capitalize on the agitation and dissatisfaction regarding the serious shortcomings in provisions for old-age security.

After 1939 the influence exerted by the Townsend movement in social security policies was comparatively less; it did not have the "political eminence" it had in the previous years—it "ceased to be a meaningful alternative in the field of social security reform." How-

ever, it is important to note that, even up to the 1950's, the Townsendites continued to be a force functioning as a background movement. [17] Despite the failure of the Townsend Movement to achieve its goal—the adoption of the Townsend Plan—its organizational weakness and other limitations, it did more to "dramatize the plight of the aged" than perhaps "any other force in American life," and in so doing exerted a continuing influence on Social Security policies. [18] Its impact on the public was such that it opened the way to acceptance of the idea of old-age protection as a matter of right, to recognizing the need for adequate benefits and to acknowledgment of the role of government in ensuring old-age security.

The Women's Social Reform Movements

Among the women's reform movements campaigning for policy changes in Social Security, leading to liberalization and extension of coverage, were the League of Women Voters, the Women's Trade Union League, the Women's Joint Congressional Committee, and the National Consumers' League. The Women's Joint Congressional Committee focused primarily on legislative activity—including Social Security legislation. It was an influential and representative committee, with which several national women's organizations were affiliated. The other women's reform movements mentioned concentrated on both educational and legislative activity. However their main emphasis was on educational and interpretive work. It should be noted that—unlike the Townsend Movement and the American Association for Social Security—the women's reform movements, the labor movement, the American Association of Social Workers and the American Public Welfare Association did not put all their efforts into campaigns for policy changes and improvements in Social Security and social insurance which were in no sense their primary interest; rather, they focused attention on a few related areas, including Social Security, within a broad spectrum of legislative concerns.

The League of Women Voters had in a sense been associated with developments in the Social Security program from its inception, in that Miss Belle Sherwin, a former President of the League, had served with the Advisory Council of President Roosevelt's Committee on Economic Security, which considered the type of social security system to be introduced. In 1934, the national board of the League of Women Voters had decided to give active support to three policy concerns which were embodied in subsequent Social Security legislation—unemployment compensation, improvements in maternal and child health, and the merit system. At the time the Social Security bill was being considered in Congress, the League, in cooperation with other groups, helped to organize mass meetings to familiarize the public with the provisions and the policy issues. [19] At the Congressional hearings held on the proposed Social Security Act, representatives of the League, Mrs. Harris T. Baldwin, Vice-President of the League, and Mrs. Beatrice Pitney Lamb, Chairman of its Department of Government and Economic Welfare, testified before the House and Senate Committees in support of the maternal and child health, and the unemployment compensation provisions of the bill.

The *News Letter* published by the League of Women Voters kept members and others informed about Social Security policy issues and legislative developments. In specific legislative situations, LWV's national office stimulated state Leagues to act. In March 1937, for example, Marguerite Wells, national President of the League, wrote to all the state League presidents urging action in connection with pending legislation which posed threats to the "merit principle." The Senate had passed the appropriation bill for the independent agencies with a "rider" which required all experts on the Social Security Board receiving $5,000.00 a year or more to be presidential appointees, subject to ratification by the Senate. This implied a return to the "spoils system" of appointment contrary to the House proposal to place Social Security experts under Civil Service.

LWV's President, in her letter urging state League presidents to act on this issue, recommended their contacting members of the

House and Senate Committees who were to confer and report back to House and Senate whether or not the rider should remain. She stated in her letter:

I suggest that, if any member of this conference committee represents your state, you as president of your state league, send him a telegram, urging the elimination of the rider from the bill because it breaks down the merit principle in the administration of the Social Security Act. [20]

There were other strategies suggested by her, such as persuading individuals who were known to have considerable influence with any of the conferees to wire them, urging the adoption of the merit system to ensure sound administration of the Social Security program. Request was also made that letters be written by citizens to the Senators from their state irrespective of whether they were on the conference committee or not. There was immediate response to the national President's request. The President of the Illinois League of Women Voters, for example, sent out a circular letter to the membership urging prompt action. [21] She reasoned that it was the League's view that Social Security services should be administered by "the highest caliber personnel," that the House proposal was a real advance in the application of the merit system, and that the Senate rider should be removed. Specific suggestions were made to wire Senators J. Hamilton Lewis and William H. Dietrich urging them to concur with the House proposal.

In 1939 when amendments were proposed providing for an increase in funds for aid to dependent children programs and appointment of state personnel under the Social Security Act by a merit system, the League gave strong support to these changes and worked for their passage. In general the League of Women Voters tended to focus more on the child welfare aspects of the Social Security bill and its amendments. However, they did give support to proposals for improvements in social insurance—specifically, extension of coverage to new groups. The League worked closely with other organizations

in the effort to bring about policy changes in Social Security, notably the National Consumers' League, the National Women's Trade Union League and the American Public Welfare Association.

The National Women's Trade Union League, essentially a federation of trade unions with women members, also showed considerable interest in policy issues and changes in Social Security during the time of the passage of the Act in 1935 and in subsequent years. They had continued to campaign for amendments to the Act to provide for extensions in coverage, increases in benefits, and the introduction of disability benefits. An area of special concern in social insurance to which the National Women's Trade Union League addressed itself was the reduction in the age of women to enable them to take full advantage of benefit payments. The President of the Women's Trade Union League of Chicago—a League representing 50,000 affiliated trade union women and auxiliary members—for example, wrote in January 1948 to Robert Ball, Director of Staff, Advisory Council on Social Security, urging improvements in the OASI provisions. Among the changes suggested was the reduction in benefit payment for women to age sixty.

The Women's Joint Congressional Committee (WJCC), consisting of delegates and representatives of several women's organizations, directed its attention to legislative activity, including changes in Social Security legislation. They showed an active interest in the passage of the Social Security Act and its subsequent amendments. The Committee on Social Security of the WJCC kept in touch with developments in Social Security legislation, and alerted members to take action as necessary. The Committee played an active part in securing the passage of the amendments of 1950. In February 1948, for example, the Committee sent a letter to Harold Knutson, Chairman, House Ways and Means Committee, with a copy to Daniel A. Reed, Chairman of the Subcommittee on Social Security, urging action for extension of Social Security provisions. The letter stated:

> The national organizations who are signatories to this letter are deeply concerned over the millions of workers, self-employed

persons, and their families, who remain unprotected by the provisions of our national Social Security Act. Our members are urging that action be taken to extend the coverage of the law and to increase the benefits, which are completely inadequate in this period of rising prices. [22]

In 1950, when the bill, H.R. 6000, which provided for amendments to the Social Security Act, was considered in the House and later in the Senate, the WJCC Committee on Extension of Social Security was alert to make representations and to work with other groups in pushing for maximum possible improvements. Prior to the Senate Finance Committee's open hearings on the bill, the WJCC Committee on Extension of Social Security met with Wilbur Cohen, Counsel to Social Security Administrator, and Elizabeth Wickenden, Washington representative of the American Public Welfare Association to discuss "problems and prospects relative to the bill," and to consider tactics and strategies to be adopted by the different organizations working for improvements in Social Security. [23]

Reference has been made to the work of the National Consumers' League in furthering improvements and changes in social insurance in the previous chapter. Apart from representations made at Congressional hearings urging liberalization and extension of the social security program, they were also active in educational programs, along with other groups, to make legislative issues known to a wider public. The most outstanding effort was the initiative taken by the League in calling an Emergency Citizens' Conference on Social Security prior to the 1954 amendments, to protect and improve the contributory social insurance system in the face of serious threats from the Curtis–Chamber of Commerce proposals. Here, as well as elsewhere, the National Consumers' League also played an important role in cooperation with other reform movements.

American Association for Social Security

The Secretary of the American Association for Social Security (AASS), Abraham Epstein, was in a sense the chief spokesman for

the social insurance concept and the most outspoken critic of Social Security programs and plans that did not go far enough or were "crackpot" schemes. As mentioned earlier, he worked untiringly for the cause of social insurance both before and after the passage of the Social Security Act, urging the utilization of the social insurance device as a means for the redistribution of wealth. Until his death in 1942 he was the most persistent critic of the existing insurance provisions and the champion of a more radical program with greater emphasis on the "social" aspects of insurance.

Epstein's criticisms of the existing social insurance programs and those associated with policy decisions, while often extreme and uncompromising, nevertheless helped to move the cause of social insurance forward. It was not enough, he argued, merely to pass the Social Security Act—it was at best a declaration of intent. It had to be implemented effectively and progressively changed. He was constantly pushing for more liberal benefit payments, extension of coverage and government contributions. Commenting on the serious limitations of the Act of 1935 and the need to carry it forward, Epstein argued that it merely set up "a system of compulsory payments by poor Paul for impoverished Peter." [24]

Epstein remained to the very end an uncompromising and controversial person in the social insurance movement. However, he provided an opportunity through the medium of AASS for a nucleus of persons concerned with improvements to come together and to exert influence on social insurance policies. [25] There were liberal economists and other social reformers—particularly Eveline Burns, Paul Douglas, Douglas Brown, Arthur Altmeyer and Wilbur Cohen—who were closely associated with him and the work of the American Association for Social Security. The AASS oficial publication, *Social Security,* and the national conferences of the Association helped to direct attention to Social Security policy issues and necessary changes.

While Epstein had close relations with such Social Security Administration staff personnel as Arthur Altmeyer, Wilbur Cohen and John Corson, he continued to prod the Social Security Adminis-

tration from outside, at times with unjustified criticism, indirectly helping to pave the way for changes. The following song sung at one of the social occasions associated with the 15th National Conference on Social Security gives some insights, in a humorous way, into the possible relationship between the Social Security Board and the American Association for Social Security. It went as follows:

> God help the S. S. Board
> Sad and forlorn
> How he rides 'em
> Their every deed
> Will but breed
> Epstein's scorn
> They get retorts
> To their reports
> They just don't go far enough.... [26]

The contents of this song composed for a social occasion in all probability distorted what might have been the real relationship between the Social Security Board and Epstein. However, the very fact that this was sung provides some clues to understanding the nature of the relationship. It is also a fact that the Social Security Board and its Chairman, Arthur Altmeyer, adopted a conscious policy of using forces adverse or critical, insofar as possible, to carry progressive policies forward. Edwin Witte, for instance, on more than one occasion responded to what he termed Epstein's unfair criticisms or "mistatements," by attempting to present the Social Security Administration's point of view and seeking support for the policies adopted by the Board. The very controversy stirred by Epstein at times led to more public effort to understand the real issues eventually leading to improvements and policy changes. It is interesting to note Edwin Witte's strong comments in a letter to the editor of the *New York Times*, attempting to correct "the misstatements" and the attacks on the Social Security system by Epstein and the AASS. Witte wrote, "To all intents and purposes Mr. Epstein is the American Association for Social Security." He went on to say

that the public should realize that the Social Security Association is really Abraham Epstein, Inc., and that statements issued in its name should be appraised accordingly. [27] Controversial and uncompromising, yet the most persistent supporter of the movement for social insurance, Epstein never relented in pushing for reforms in old-age and survivors' insurance, unemployment insurance and the enactment of a health insurance program.

American Public Welfare Association

The American Public Welfare Association (APWA) was an informal partner of the federal government in the effective administration of Social Security programs, and in bringing about necessary changes and improvements. The power base of APWA was essentially the Council of State Administrators. APWA mobilized state officials for support of policies and changes in the public welfare field, including social security. While APWA may not have been powerful enough to put through legislation, it was in a position to prevent legislation that was regressive and to provide feedbacks regarding necessary changes based on experience in administering programs. In this sense it was an important force.

While public assistance was the specialty of APWA, it gave attention to social insurance as well. Extension of social insurance coverage, it was felt, would lessen the public assistance costs and the caseloads that the states would have to bear; for this reason alone extensions in social insurance seemed desirable. The preventive approach to the problem of dependency embodied in social insurance provided a further impetus. In the extension of coverage, particularly to farmers and the self-employed, the APWA played an important role.

APWA's Washington office and its *Washington News Letter* helped to highlight legislative developments pertaining to Social Security, relief and related matters and kept its members and friends informed about policy issues and changes. When amendments to the Social Security Act were considered in Congress, the *News Letter*

served as a channel of communication to clarify issues, alert members to necessary action, and to give indications of "off the record" thinking and "behind the scene" maneuvers. The APWA annual round table conferences, regional conferences and institutes also afforded opportunities for discussing the working of the Social Security programs and the policy changes considered desirable.

In this respect, the role of Elizabeth Wickenden, the APWA Washington representative, who served the association for over ten years between 1941 and 1951, is noteworthy. She helped to establish close links between APWA and organized labor, the women's reform movements and the American Association of Social Workers to encourage joint action on Social Security policy issues and needed changes. The effectiveness of these combined efforts was most evident in their support of H.R. 6000 which provided for the amendments of 1950.

The APWA *News Letter* of March 15, 1950, for example, alerted its readers to the fact that the Senate Finance Committee was likely to report a more conservative version of H.R. 6000 than that passed by the House, emphasizing the need to put pressure on Senators to propose and support more liberal provisions. Wickenden went on to indicate in this particular *News Letter* some of the controversial policy questions confronting the Senate Finance Committee, such as: Should the social insurance system be made comprehensive by extending coverage to farm workers and self-employed farmers? Should the insurance system include protection against permanent and total disability? What should be the maximum insurance benefit level? And, how much additional money could the federal government make available to the states in meeting welfare needs? [28]

APWA's Welfare Policy Committee made its contribution in paving the way for the introduction of the 1950 amendments, as well as other Social Security changes, in the continuous questioning and adoption of a policy stand, and in making it known to a wider public. In the 1949 objectives for public welfare legislation, for example, the Welfare Policy Committee gave major emphasis to the final point of its twelve-point platform, dealing with the prevention

of dependency through extension of the contributory social insurance principle. The Committee indicated that not only was action on the insurance program of primary importance for its own sake, but also that "legislative action in the area of public welfare" could be carried forward only if the existent pressures on assistance programs were first relieved by extension and liberalization of social insurance. [29] APWA was able to mobilize strong support for policy changes leading to extension of social insurance from state governors and administrators, both conservative and liberal, who were basically motivated by the selfish interest of reducing public assistance expenditure and responsibility at the state level.

American Association of Social Workers

In a sense the American Association of Social Workers (AASW), a professional organization of persons in public welfare and private social work, was the main channel for making known social workers' thinking, approach to specific social problems, and stands on policy matters during the 1935-1954 period. There were also other organizations of varying influence, such as the National Federation of Settlements and Neighborhood Centers and the National Social Welfare Assembly. Reference has already been made to the role of the American Public Welfare Association. The National Conference of Social Work, and such journals as *Survey* and *The Compass* were also valuable media for disseminating the thinking and approach to social problems by social workers and social reformers.

The primary objective of AASW, founded in 1917, was the ensuring of professional standards for social work. This was the main emphasis in its activities, especially in the early years. Consideration of social policy changes, particularly in the area of social insurance, was a later development. This is not to imply that there was a lack of concern in this area, but rather that this was not given a heavy emphasis in the organization's priorities. Individual social workers in collaboration with social reformers, however, were active in the cause of social insurance and in policy issues and changes.

Social workers had been active in shaping Federal Emergency Relief Administration programs in the 1930's, but they did not play an equally active role regarding social insurance, especially in its early stages. This is partly to be explained by their preoccupation with meeting immediate and pressing needs, and providing treatment services. Social workers were also more experienced in relief and assistance work than in the area of social insurance. However, this did not connote a lack of concern for or interest in social insurance and related policy questions. During the 1935-1954 period, it is evident that the American Association of Social Workers—especially individual social workers with expertise in Social Security and related programs—became progressively involved in policy issues and changes.

At the AASW conference in 1937, William Hodson had asked social workers to familiarize themselves with social insurance programs and needed changes:

> ... By and large the experience of social workers has been in the area of relief and assistance. It is in this area that the organized social work group speaks with the broadest knowledge and competence. While there are many social workers who are social scientists in a broader sense and are therefore qualified as individuals to speak authoritatively with regard to the social insurances, this is probably not true of the profession as a whole. Nevertheless, we are conscious of the close inter-relationship between the public assistance and the insurance provisions of the Social Security Act and the constant relation and interaction between the two, and there is certainly an obligation resting upon all of us to familiarize ourselves as fully as possible with the special insurances as we have never done before. [30]

Hodson urged that changes be made in the Social Security Act, extending coverage as broadly as possible, including nonprofit agencies and employees of state and local governments. He also stressed the need to amend the Act to establish minimum standards for the selection of personnel on a merit basis, a principle that AASW was

bound to emphasize with its commitment to the goal of improved standards in administration and practice. Another policy change advocated, but not implemented (however, meriting consideration even today), was the elimination of compulsory payments of tax towards old-age benefits by employees with annual earnings of less than a thousand dollars. This was based on the argument that they required all of the limited annual earnings to maintain a minimum standard of living. [31]

A few months after the AASW conference of 1937, Walter West, Executive Secretary of AASW, wrote individual members of the newly appointed Advisory Council on Social Security to propose discussion of likely social security changes in the future. [32] This was done especially on behalf of AASW's Division on Government and Social Work, which had a particular interest in working for improvements in Social Security. This Advisory Council, as mentioned in Chapter 3, was appointed in 1937 jointly by the Social Security Board and the Special Committee on Social Security of the Senate Finance Committee, and had terms of reference sufficiently broad to deal with important policy questions.

The Executive Secretary of AASW also served as Chairman of the National Committee on Inclusion of Social Work Agencies under the Social Security Act in 1937. The primary efforts of this committee were directed to introducing changes to the Act to ensure that social agencies under private auspices were subject to the Act's provisions on the same basis as industrial and commercial enterprises. Here the social work agencies were essentially representing their own interests. While it was not possible to introduce this change in the 1939 amendments, it did become effective under a subsequent amendment. However, the efforts of social workers and others to include recognition in the 1939 amendments of the "merit principle" in administration, basic in improving social welfare programs, proved to be successful.

In earlier chapters, reference has been made to AASW representations at Congressional hearings, held before the different amendments were introduced, urging improvements in Social Security

programs and policy changes. In addition, AASW engaged in educational efforts to publicize policy issues and needed changes. In May 1949, for example, it issued a declaration, "A Social Policy for Today," which included policy statements on social assistance and social insurance adopted in 1948. [33] Prior to the 1954 amendments, Elizabeth Wickenden, AASW Consultant on Public Social Policy, helped to focus attention on social security policy issues and needed action, through her writings in the *Public Social Policy Bulletin*, and in serving as a resource for various organizations interested in Social Security changes. It is interesting to note that, in January 1954, the AASW Committee on Public Social Policy, discussing the basic points of AASW strategy, was of the opinion that the Association should center its major legislative interest in the field of Social Security, "with first priority given to the strengthening of the old-age and survivors' insurance program." [34] The AASW also offered the services of its Washington representative and its consultants to other organizations in an offer to work together in pushing for Social Security policy changes.

However, AASW and other social work organizations had no major political thrust in the push for Social Security policy changes as compared, for instance, with organized labor. Social workers were a constructive force, sometimes taking neutral positions to encourage opposing groups to join forces to act in behalf of progressive policy changes. There are evidences of cooperation between social work and the labor movement in regard to particular legislative changes in social insurance, with the Social Security Board serving as the rallying point. But in the main, social work's contribution was more evident in providing the necessary expertise in formulating proposals for changes in Social Security policies and programs.

Social policy changes in Social Security—specifically, social insurance—emerged as a result of the interaction of several factors, one such being the influence exerted by the social reform movements. It is difficult to assess in exact terms the particular influence of each of the reform movements studied. An attempt has been made insofar as possible, based on available data, to indicate the nature of the efforts

made by the respective reform movements to bring about changes in Social Security through lobbying and related work, as well as educational efforts.

Undoubtedly, the impact of a particular reform movement on policy decisions in the area of social insurance varied, depending on its resources and the nature of the priority it assigned to social security. Such reform movements as the American Association for Social Security and the Townsend Movement focused almost exclusively on social security—specifically old-age security, whereas others had Social Security as but one important area of interest.

Even when they had Social Security as an important area of interest, in one or two instances they were more concerned with policy changes in public assistance or child welfare provisions of the Social Security Act. Also, while such reform movements as labor had an ongoing and progressively increasing interest in Social Security policy changes, with others, such as the American Association for Social Security and the Townsend Movement, there was a diminishing interest and influence in the later years.

It is clear that the reform movements differed in their tactics to influence policy changes. Organized labor, for example, had a heavy emphasis on lobbying and related work, whereas other organizations, such as the American Association of Social Workers and the American Public Welfare Association, gave greater weight to educational efforts. Collectively, however, the varied efforts of the several reform movements represented a force in the arena of Social Security policy making that could not be ignored.

NOTES

1. Altmeyer, *op. cit.*, p. 32.
2. Lubove, *op. cit.*, pp. 15-16.
3. Bremner, *op. cit.*, p. 263.
4. Hofstadter. *The Age of Reform, op. cit.*, p. 308.
5. Letter from Nelson H. Cruikshank to Mathew Woll, August 11, 1955, Mathew Woll, Box 6A, *Nelson Cruikshank Papers.* Manuscripts Library, State Historical Society of Wisconsin.

6. Letter from William Green, President AFL to President Roosevelt, June 22, 1937, File 011.4 July-December 1937, *Central Files of the Social Security Board, 1935-1947*, National Archives, Record Group 47, Washington, D.C.

7. Reply of President Roosevelt to William Green, President, AFL, July 6, 1937, *ibid.*

8. Interview by the author with Arthur J. Altmeyer, Madison, Wisconsin, October 29, 1970.

9. See Abraham Holtzman. *The Townsend Movement: A Political Study.* New York: Bookman Associates, Inc., 1963, pp. 40-46.

10. *Ibid.*, p. 15.

11. *Ibid.*, p. 86.

12. For a psychological analysis of the Townsend scheme, see Hadley Cantril. *The Psychology of Social Movements.* New York: John Wiley and Sons, Inc., 1967, pp. 169-209.

13. Song, "The Townsend Plan," sung at the Townsend mass meeting of November 4, 1934, Townsend Plan, Box 43, *The Records of the Committee on Economic Security*, National Archives, Group 47, Washington D.C.

14. Holtzman, *op. cit.*, p. 48.

15. *Ibid.*, p. 201.

16. Letter from Edwin Witte to Abraham Epstein, September 15, 1938. American Association for Social Security 1938, Box 43, *Edwin E. Witte Papers*, Manuscripts Library, State Historical Society of Wisconsin.

17. Interview by the author with Charles I. Schottland; Brandeis University, Waltham, Mass., September 21, 1970.

18. Holtzman, *op. cit.*, p. 202.

19. League of Women Voters and the Social Security Act, Social Security Bill 1935-1936, Box 347-1934-1936, *League of Women Voters Papers*, Manuscript Division, Library of Congress, Washington, D.C.

20. Letter from Marquerite Wells, President, National League of Women Voters, March 3, 1937, to State League Presidents, Social Security Rider, 1936-1938, Box 377, *League of Women Voters Papers*, Manuscript Division, Library of Congress, Washington, D.C.

21. Circular letter from Alice Hixon, President, Illinois League of Women Voters, March 4, 1937, to State League members, *Ibid.*

22. Report of Social Security Committee, Minutes of Women's Joint Congressional Committee 3.1.1948, Box 8, *Women's Joint Congressional Committee Papers*, Manuscript Division, Library of Congress, Washington, D.C.

23. Extension of Social Security, Minutes of Women's Joint Congressional Committee, 1.9.1950. Minutes 1950, *Ibid.*

24. Abraham Epstein. "Our Social Insecurity Act," *Harper's Magazine.* Harper and Brothers Publishers, December 1935, p. 65.

25. Interview by author with Dr. Eveline Burns; New York, September 15, 1970.

26. Songs for Epstein's Party 4/11/1942, American Association for Social Security, Box 26, *Epstein Papers*, Labor Management and Document Center, New York State School of Industrial and Labor Relations, Cornell University.

27. Edwin E. Witte, Letter to the Editor, *New York Times* 1/6/1937; File 095. E.E. Witte 1937, Records of the Chairman, Social Security Board 1935-1940, National Archives, Record Group 47, Washington D.C.

28. American Public Welfare Association; Letter to Members, March 15, 1950.

29. Statement of Welfare Policy Committee. "Public Welfare Platform:

Objectives for Public Welfare Legislation in 1949." APWA, 1949, p. 3. (Reprinted from the March 1949 issue of *Public Welfare.*)

30. William Hodson. "Current Problems of Government and Social Work," *The Compass.* March, 1937, p. 13. Note: The text of Hodson's talk as Chairman, National Division on Government and Social Work, AASW, appeared in *The Compass,* under the above title.

31. *Ibid.*

32. Letter from Walter West, Executive Secretary, AASW, to Lucy Mason, National Consumers' League, 5/.7/1937, Social Security Correspondence 1937-38, 4NN-1 *National Consumers' League Papers,* Manuscript Division, Library of Congress, Washington D.C.

33. "A Social Policy for Today," *American Association of Social Workers,* New York, May 1949.

34. Memo by Elizabeth Wickenden, American Association of Social Workers, 1/18/1954; Social Security, *Elizabeth Wickenden Papers* 1954, Manuscripts Library, State Historical Society of Wisconsin.

V

An Evaluation of the Reform Movements' Efforts to Influence Policy Changes

It is increasingly evident that there is no issue on which the American people are more genuinely united than that of improving our social insurance system. . . . Labor's problem in securing passage of social security legislation is to make this demand articulate and to make it heard in the halls of Congress.

Nelson Cruikshank in an article, "H.R. 6000 and You," reprinted from *The American Federationist*, October 1949.

I sometimes wonder whether our devotion to a cause may have the effect of narrowing our point of view until we are unable to take a broad enough outlook on the world as a whole, to have the proper perspective on our particular interest.

Yet on the other hand, the drive of the person with the restricted interest is desperately needed to move almost any cause forward against the apathetic attitude taken by most people.

Mrs. Franklin Roosevelt, commenting on Dr. Townsend's visit to the White House in her "My Day" column, *Washington Daily News*, March 27, 1940.

157

Relative Effectiveness of the Diverse Approaches

ANY ATTEMPT to examine critically the various attempts to influence policy changes in social insurance, and to assess the relative effectiveness of the reform movements, is fraught with serious difficulties. Even if it is possible to identify and to analyze the different efforts, there are no adequate answers to questions such as: Is it possible to determine specifically what impact a particular effort had in influencing policy? Or, in the interaction of several forces leading to policy changes, how precisely is it possible to assess the influence of a particular effort, by a single organization, at a given time? Despite the obvious difficulties in making such evaluations, some judgments based on available evidence are called for, hopefully—insofar as possible—free from bias.

It will be noted from the discussions in the preceding chapters that the reform movements' diverse efforts to effect policy changes in social insurance were in two broad areas of activity, educational work and lobbying and related work. The nature of the tactics used to influence policy changes depended to some extent on the nature of the organization themselves, their resources, objectives and priorities. Each of the reform organizations and interest groups that we have examined had the specific goal of bringing about changes in services provided or institutional changes, in social welfare and related fields. Such social reform movements as the labor movement and the Townsend Movement aimed equally at institutional and basic policy changes, and relied heavily on lobbying and other forms of political activity to bring about policy changes. Such organizations as the American Association of Social Workers and the American Public Welfare Association were more concerned with policy in relation to changes in service delivery, and focused more on educational efforts likely to influence policy changes.

As we have already seen, every reform movement, irrespective of

its particular interest or priority, resorted to various educational methods to disseminate information, interpret issues and influence policy decisions. These included periodic press releases, newsletters, memoranda, bulletins, pamphlets and journals.

Reference has already been made to such public educational efforts as the press releases by labor and other groups on policy questions, the *Townsend Weekly* and its campaigns, the newsletters of the national League of Women Voters, the AASW's *Public Social Policy Bulletin* and articles in the *APWA Journal* and in *Social Security,* the official publication of the American Association for Social Security, to mention only a few. But the important question remains: How effectively were they utilized, and what was the extent of their contribution to affecting public thinking and attitudes, and to building support for progressive Social Security policies? Needless to say, there are no exact answers to these questions, however important; at best there can be some useful explorations.

The effectiveness of these educational efforts in influencing public opinion and policy depended on how often they were utilized, what kind of an audience they attempted to reach and to what extent they targeted in on specific issues, on bills being voted on, and on guidelines for action by members and friends of the movements. The size of the organization's membership, the ongoing sustained nature of its educational effort and the wider public to whom educational efforts were directed—these and other related factors— are important considerations in determining effectiveness. The labor movement, for example, had the largest membership and a more sustained interest in Social Security policy changes, invested relatively greater resources in educational and interpretive efforts. It could therefore be argued that the educational and interpretive efforts made by labor would have been more effective.

This does not imply that only the size of membership and the sustained character of the educational efforts, in and of themselves, ensured success. There were other determinants of effectiveness, such as the nature of the current leadership, competent staff for research and information services, sound judgment in selecting the

particular type of educational medium to be used, and the degree of specificity or generality desirable in focusing on policy issues in a particular context. Both the AFL and CIO had, for example, competent research and information services, and it is evident that the Socail Security Board observed closely the educational efforts, thinking, and proposals for change that emerged from labor. The Social Security policy changes recommended at the annual conventions of the AFL, and the CIO board resolutions and similar policy declarations of other organizations were studied carefully by officials of the Social Security Board. This is just one example of the Board's effort to keep in close touch with labor and similar groups, as indicated by President Roosevelt in his letter of July 6, 1937 to William Green.

The educational programs of APWA, AASW, and some of the women's reform movements were aimed primarily at their own members with the intent of influencing public opinion through them. The possibility of reaching others closely related was always there and was also explored. APWA and AASW were professional organizations whose major *raison d'être* was improved standards and more effective delivery of services. Educational efforts, however, were directed towards keeping the membership and others informed about Social Security policy issues and necessary program changes. Guidelines for action were also suggested, but it is difficult to ascertain with any precision the extent to which they were implemented and the nature of the impact that these efforts had on public opinion.

Other forms of educational activity aimed at stimulating public discussion on Social Security policies and proposals. In addition to their news releases, there were also articles and letters to the editor in newspapers. Talks and discussions were also held on radio and television, in schools and forum groups. The American Forum of the Air, for example, presented a panel discussion on Social Security and the Townsend Plan. [1] Special public meetings and conferences on needed changes in Social Security programs reached additional audiences. Opportunities for debate and exchange of views were afforded

by the National Conference of Social Work, the National Conference of the American Association for Social Security, the APWA Annual Round Table Conference, the Annual Convention of Labor, and the Townsend Convention. However, differences arose out of the very nature of each group's meeting, and affected the kind of impact their thinking and discussion had on the public.

The APWA and NCSW conferences served mainly as a forum for professionals engaged in private social work and public welfare, affording opportunities for debating Social Security policy and problems. Arthur Altmeyer, for example, addressed the NCSW in 1953 on Social Security changes following the presentation by Congressman Carl Curtis who had given the famous Curtis-Chamber of Commerce proposals for regressive policy changes.

However, it should be pointed out that the impact that these periodic conferences of professionals had on the wider public was limited when compared with that of the labor conventions, or the Townsend conventions up to 1939. They were much smaller groups and, as William Hodson candidly observed in the AASW conference of 1937, social workers were more experienced in the area of relief and assistance work than in social insurance programs and policies.

Special study groups and committees were set up within organizations, utilizing a nucleus of people capable of analyzing Social Security policy issues, evaluating existing programs and recommending needed changes. Where such groups worked together they were evidently more effective. APWA and AASW did not have a sufficient power base to push for policy changes on their own, but they could study selectively the working of existing programs and the possible impact of new programs, and could be a resource in this way to ther groups. [2] The AASW Division of Government and Social Work, for example, strove to work closely with the Social Security Board to suggest changes on the basis of studies and surveys undertaken—hopefully in this way to influence policy decisions.

The Social Security Board and its officials, notably Arthur Altmeyer and Wilbur Cohen, played key roles in maintaining close contact with the reform groups, providing the necessary leadership

from within the Administration, and utilizing outside resources to bring about progressive changes in Social Security. Members of the Social Security Board were invited to attend sessions of the AASW Division of Government and Social Work. Likewise, Miss Dorothy Kahn, Chairman of AASW, along with other AASW representatives met with members of the Social Security Board to share the findings of a survey conducted by the Association and the concerns arising from it—specifically the need for extension of coverage. [3] It was spokesmen from public welfare and social work who, on the basis of experience with programs and projections, emphasized one of the most convincing reasons for extension of insurance coverage—the lowering of public assistance costs. This was a timely additional argument that labor and other groups seized upon to campaign for extension of social insurance coverage to farm workers and self-employed farmers in rural areas. [4]

At the same time, the AASS nucleus of persons competent and knowledgeable in Social Security matters, through their writings, their contributions at national conferences of their own and other related organizations, attempted to bring needed policy changes into focus. These persons acted as an outside force bringing pressure to bear on the Social Security Board for policy changes. Abraham Epstein, as AASS's Executive Secretary, played a dominant role in establishing the Act of 1935 and its 1939 amendments. The very criticisms and controversies that he stirred up seemed to bring Social Security policy issues into the open for a wider public seeking to understand the real issues.

It was here that the role of Altmeyer, Witte, Cohen and others, in providing factual data, disagreeing with unfounded criticism and pointing to needed action, helped immensely in keeping the public informed and in enlisting support for greater liberalization of Social Security programs. Epstein was pushing for more fundamental changes based on the contributory principle, such as government contribution and the use of social insurance as an important device for redistribution of income. The advocacy of these radical changes, basically within the social insurance framework, had the effect of

loosening the grip of conservative forces delaying progressive developments. After Epstein's death in 1942, however, the influence of AASS diminished appreciably.

Efforts of the reform movements and related groups to influence Social Security changes were in no sense restricted to the national level. We have already cited, for example, the newsletters and personal letters from the President of the national League of Women Voters to Presidents of state Leagues, urging specific action on Social Security bills then pending. Similar attempts to reach their members at state and local levels were made by the unions, APWA, AASW and the Townsend Movement. APWA was active in mobilizing state officials to back extension of OASI coverage to farm workers and the self-employed, and increased benefit payments. APWA exercised pressure at the state level by writing personal letters to and seeing state political leaders and officials.

As noted earlier, the interest of state governors and administrators in reducing state responsibility for public assistance expenditure was a key factor exploited by labor, APWA and other groups in pushing for extension of social insurance coverage to new groups.

As would be expected, where the national organizations had support at the grassroots level their attempts to influence policy were more effective. But again the nature of the organization, the size of its membership, the extent of political support and influence were determinants. APWA's and AASW's primary emphasis on educational efforts seemed to be most effective when carried out in collaboration with other groups.

Reform movements that attempted to influence policy through lobbying and related activity, in addition to educational efforts, are likely to have had a greater impact. The availability of alternative methods of influencing policy and the choice of the appropriate method or methods at a given time, in a given situation, were basic to their success. Labor, the League of Women Voters, and the National Consumers' League urged adoption of specific Social Security planks in the Democratic and Republican party platforms—an effective means of influencing Social Security legislation. In his

testimony at the hearings before the House Ways and Means Committee prior to adoption of the 1946 amendments, James Carey, Secretary-Treasurer of the CIO, made reference to the Social Security planks in both Democratic and Republican Platforms of 1944, and urged legislators of both parties to fulfill their respective campaign promises.

Similarly, writing to the President and to Congressmen had optimum effect when passage or defeat of a bill was at a crucial stage. In the conference stage of particular bills, the sustained efforts of both labor and the League of Women Voters were of strategic value, and merit special attention. Where representations at Congressional hearings were concentrated on specific issues, and where representations were made before both the House and Senate Committees, efforts were likely to be most effective. Often the introduction of a bill providing for Social Security changes generated active interest and representatives of reform movements would appear before the House Ways and Means Committee to support the changes; but, unfortunately, when the bill was before the Senate Finance Committee, where attempts were being made to dilute or eliminate some of the progressive features that had been approved by the House, there would be no equal show of strength from the reform movements.

The Townsend Movement utilized the election campaigns in attempts to influence Social Security policies and to push for its own plan by pressure-group endorsements of sympathetic candidates. This was particularly evident, just prior to enactment of the 1939 amendments, when more than ninety Republicans who had professed some commitment to the Townsend Plan were elected to Congress (in November 1938), and constituted over one-half of the Republican members in the House. [5] The question arises as to how effective the Townsend Movement was in influencing social security policies through such pressure-group endorsements. It has been seen that the inclusion of the old-age insurance provisions in the Social Security Act in 1935 was due largely to the Townsend pressure. The Townsend Movement is said to have "crystallized" popular sentiment in favor of old-age security. The threat of more

fundamental change posed by the Townsend plan weakened conservative opposition to the relatively moderate proposals introduced by the Act. [6] The Townsend Movement continued to be a force for further liberalization of social security policies by the very threat of its own plan—even after 1935 and particularly in the 1939 amendments. Some groups, such as the General Welfare Federation, dropped out of the Townsend Movement but continued to work for Social Security betterment.

The Townsend Movement itself eventually ceased being a national organization, but there were state groups, strongest in Colorado and California, pushing for changes in Social Security and related areas. [7] Among the reform movements, the Townsend's was the one organization predominantly composed of the aged, the very persons directly affected by OASI policies. In this sense it had the potential of a powerful self-interest group. It was a "depression phenomenon," and when the basic need of security for the elderly seemed to have been provided for by alternative means, there was no receptivity to plans such as Townsend's.

Critics point out that the failure of the Townsend lobby in Congress is largely attributable to the inability of the national organization to function effectively as a political machine. [8] A major political drawback of the Townsend movement was its inability to develop a "coherent endorsement policy" due to inept leadership and loose organization. The Townsendites were known to make claims after each election that many of their endorsed candidates were elected, but it was never certain whether such candidates were actually committed to the plan or would give even minimum support. On those rare occasions when this was put to the test, there were disastrous consequences for the Townsend Plan. [9]

The Townsend endorsement records are reported to reveal "a contradictory, self-negative policy," in that while efforts were made to obtain definite commitments for the Townsend Plan from candidates, there was little, if any, follow-through. Close working relationships with the Congressmen they had helped to elect, and leadership in utilizing their support resourcefully, so basic to effective lobbying

work, was lacking—in constrast, for example, to the part played by organized labor in post-election lobbying. Labor revealed greater leadership skills, and worked closely with its allies in Congress, particularly Democratic Congressmen, to support more liberal social security policies.

The Townsend Plan and Movement were identified in name, origin, control and ownership with the founder, Dr. Townsend. Any questioning of policy at the grassroots level was interpreted at the national headquarters as a personal attack on Dr. Townsend's capabilities and judgment as leader. [10] This was yet another source of weakness in the movement, contributing to its overall ineffectiveness in the political arena, and its later inability to influence social security policies significantly.

In contrast to the decreasing effective influence of the Townsend Movement, the effective influence exerted by organized labor in shaping social security policies increased over the years. Where labor worked closely with the Social Security Board and with other reform movements as, for instance, in the organization of the Citizens Conference on Social Security in 1953 to meet the challenge to progressive Social Security policies posed by the Curtis-Chamber of Commerce proposals, the impact was manifestly greater. [11]

The close link between the Social Security Board and labor in working for advances in Social Security programs was also a positive factor. Evidence from memoranda and letters written by Altmeyer and other Social Security officials indicate acknowledgment of the role of labor in building support for progressive changes initiated by the administration. [12] In some instances SSB officials served as the "intelligentsia" for the labor movement, providing the background to problems, analyses of issues, and likely approaches to solutions.

During the period from 1935 to 1954, labor emerged as the dominant interest group favoring progressive changes in the Social Security Act. In the case of every key policy issue and proposal, labor was on the side of the proponents of progressive legislation and helped to guide it toward passage. The three major basic changes in

the Social Security Act—in 1939, the inclusion of survivors' benefits; in 1950, broadening coverage and improving average benefits by 77 percent; in 1954, extending coverage to ten million new workers— were all developed with the active support of labor. [13] If labor had taken a different stand, or no stand at all, it is hard to predict what the outcome would have been for the progressive policy changes formulated in the amendments to the Act.

Patterns of Cooperation or Conflict Among Reform Movements

There were, it will be noted, two main streams of thinking in regard to the institutional device to be adopted for ensuring security for the aged—one embodying the social insurance concept; the other, the universal flat pension idea. All the reform movements except Townsend's were committed to the social insurance concept. Obviously, there would have been collaboration among these reform movements in the effort to introduce progressive social security policies. To what degree there was a regular pattern of cooperation, it is hard to discern on the basis of the data available. The extent of cooperation seems to have increased prior to the enactment of each of the amendments to the Act.

There appears to have been a close working relationship among the American Public Welfare Association, League of Women Voters, National Consumers' League, National Women's Trade Union League and American Association for Social Security. The National Consumers' League, for example, was a member of the American Association for Social Security. The cooperation seems to have been task-oriented, working together for specific policy changes, such as introduction of the "merit principle," or averting the threat to the contributory principle in social insurance posed by the Curtis-Chamber of Commerce proposals in 1953.

In a sense this pattern of cooperation to affect Social Security legislation had its precedents in such events as the meeting of representatives of national organizations held in Washington, D.C. in March 1935, prior to adoption of the Social Security Act, to urge its

adoption and endorsement of the principles embodied in it. The chairman of this representative group of organizations was Grace Abbott, Professor of Public Welfare Administration at the University of Chicago, and a member of the Board of Directors of the American Public Welfare Association. Among those present were representatives of the American Public Welfare Association, League of Women Voters, American Association for Labor Legislation, and American Association of Social Workers. Representatives of this meeting carried a letter to the President, pledging support of the group in the efforts to expedite passage of the bill. [14] Likewise, a letter was sent a few days later to all members of Congress, urging the adoption of the economic security bill.

It is interesting to note that at that 1935 meeting there was considerable stress on the importance of united support for the bill and the need to end personal differences over details. Here was being formulated a pattern that continued in subsequent activities supporting policy changes and amendments to the Act. This does not imply, however, that there were no conflicts or rivalry among the organizations. As noted earlier there was rivalry even among organizations committed to the social insurance movement, notably the American Association for Labor Legislation and the American Association for Social Security—largely attributable to differences between Epstein and Andrews, personal differences as well as disagreements over policy. [15] Within the labor movement, too, there were differences between the AFL and the CIO. Despite such differences a cooperative working relationship did emerge, focusing on collective tasks.

The role of the Social Security Board in this cooperative effort among the reform movements committed to the furtherance of the social insurance programs was significant. The Board often served as a resource and a facilitator for the reform movements to mobilize their resources collectively to support progressive social security policies. As a government agency the Board could not lobby, but through its reports, testimony at public hearings, provision of technical assistance to a Senator or to an organization such as labor, it had the potential indirectly to influence policy. [16] Several factors

contributed to the SSB leadership role in initiating or winning support for social security policy changes; among them were the caliber of the staff, the built-in requirement that the Board suggest changes in policy and programs, and the research orientation permeating the entire Board. [17]

It is significant that the SSB had a special Labor Information Division which served as a two-way communications channel—to labor and from labor. This service was established in recognition of labor's stake in social security programs, and in acknowledgement of the fact that the full understanding and cooperation of labor throughout the country was essential for the development of progressive Social Security programs. [18] There were several instances where the Social Security Committee of the AFL or CIO met with SSB members at strategic times to discuss further developments in policies. [19] Arthur Altmeyer's comments on the role of labor in reviewing the first three years of operation of the Social Security program is revelatory of the nature of the relationship that had developed during that period and that was to continue. He acknowledged the counsel, criticism and cooperation extended by labor, and the SSB's and the nation's debt for such unwavering support. [20]

There were also collaborative efforts among reform movements on Social Security changes, independent of the Social Security Board's close association with organized labor. The Women's Joint Congressional Committee, which symbolized the cooperative effort of several women's organizations, concentrated on legislative activity including Social Security legislation. In March 1949, for example, Elizabeth Wickenden, Washington representative of APWA, met with the Social Security Committee of the WJCC and others to discuss action that should be taken to support legislation favoring extension and improvement of the OASI program. [21]

Among all the cooperative efforts undertaken by the social reform movements, the Citizens Conference on Social Security held in May 1953 is in many ways unique. It was a coming together of several organizations to uphold the contributory social insurance system and to ensure extension and improved benefits, at a time

when the very principle of contributory social insurance seemed jeopardized by the Curtis-Chamber of Commerce proposals. Were it not for this conference, crystallizing the support of labor and the other reform movements, it is debatable whether the 1954 amendments would have embodied the progressive changes in Social Security that they did. Indeed, at times it seemed as though the forces opposed to social insurance based on the contributory principle would succeed in introducing their regressive measures. There was a confrontation between those who wanted to continue and develop further the policy of major reliance on contributory social insurance with increased benefit payments, and those who wanted to emasculate OASI by replacing it with a universal low-level payment plan. The reform movements through the medium of the Citizens Conference on Social Security mobilized their resources to oppose the regressive proposals. Among the reform movements comprising the backbone of the Conference were the American Federation of Labor, the Congress of Industrial Organizations, the Public Welfare Association and the National Consumers' League.

There were also other significant forms of collaboration to influence policy changes in social insurance such as the informal working coalition on social security which included Elizabeth Wickenden, Wilbur Cohen, Fedele Fauri, Katherine Ellickson and Nelson Cruikshank. Despite the differences between the top leadership of the AFL and CIO, there was considerable cooperation between the Social Security staffs of both labor organizations in pushing for improvements. Both Elizabeth Wickenden and Wilbur Cohen played a key role in bringing together the different interests such as labor, public welfare and social work, in giving support to progressive Social Security policies.

While there was an appreciable amount of cooperation there were also instances of conflict. Reference has already been made to differences between the AFL and CIO in regard to labor legislation. Even within the AFL there were instances of conflict over Social Security policies. In the 1940 and 1944 conventions of the AFL, for example, sharp differences are reported to have developed on the

floor among representatives of employees of states and municipalities regarding OASI coverage. However, even in these situations, the Social Security Committee of the AFL was able to develop a compromise position which was incorporated into the law and recognized in the Amendments of 1950 and 1954. [22] There are also evidences of conflict and controversy between Epstein of the American Association for Social Security and Andrews of the American Association for Labor Legislation. Epstein was also known to attack the SSB and the administration policy, and in a sense the very controversy he stirred up brought public attention and concern for Social Security issues. Attacking the Social Security plan in a speech in 1936, for example, he stated that the Roosevelt administration's program would not protect the American people against insecurity "so long as it squeezes from them" instead of getting from inheritance and income taxes the money to finance itself. [23]

However, it was the Townsend Movement that aroused the most controversy and criticism regarding the administration's social security program, going so far as to present its plan as an alternative and, in turn, experiencing the antagonism of some of the reform movements. In his testimony before the House Ways and Means Committee in 1939, for example, Dr. Townsend asserted that the existent Social Security legislation was the height of absurdity. Spokesmen for the reform movements, economists and others in turn dubbed the Townsend Plan a "crackpot scheme." Insofar as Townsend was opposed to the contributory social insurance concept based on the wage-related principle and was advocating a universal flat-pension scheme, there was a major policy rift between his movement and the rest of the reform movements. Hence there could be no conceivable pattern of cooperation between the Townsend Movement and the other reform movements.

Even before the passage of the Social Security Act representatives of the reform movements had denounced the Townsend Plan. William Green, President of the AFL, stated that schemes like the Townsend Plan made sound legislation difficult. He went so far as to warn elderly people in general and the labor movement in particular

against being misled by such unrealistic proposals. [24] Epstein referred to the Townsend Movement cynically as the "finest promotion job in American history." The rejection of the Townsend proposals by the reform movements was also evident at the state level. A resolution favoring the Townsend Plan was rejected at the convention of the Oregon State Federation of Labor in 1938. [25] Correspondence between the Portland League of Women Voters and the national office of the League also indicates conflicts between the local League and the Townsend Movement in Oregon. [26]

There is some evidence that at least in one or two isolated instances CIO representatives were in conversation with representatives of the Townsend Movement to woo their support for the CIO Social Security proposals. A memorandum written to James Carey of the CIO following such a meeting indicates that the Townsendites were prepared to support any progressive old-age program. Joseph Kovner who wrote the memo seemed to believe that the Townsendites were changing their earlier position under the pressure of war. Whether this was in fact the case is hard to say, but it is clear that representatives of labor and the Townsend Movement did have an exploratory meeting and there was indication of a willingness to follow up on the meeting. [27]

It is also interesting to note that, during the time of the Curtis–Chamber of Commerce attack on the Social Security program in 1953, the Townsendites did not join the opponents of the existing program as was feared—or might have been expected because what was presented in the Curtis-Chamber of Commerce proposal seemed to be a "modified Townsend Plan." As the *Townsend Weekly,* commenting on it editorially put it, "the crusty, conservative, tax-conscious old c of c," had appeared to come out with a "modified Townsend Plan," but then, the editor confessed, "the unpleasant truth dawned." [28] It is a moot question whether the 1954 amendments would have gone as far as they did if the Townsendites had decided to throw in their resources on the side of the Social Security foes. A key question to ponder in this context is whether minimizing or neutralizing the sources of opposition is, at strategic times,

equally as important as enlisting support and cooperation to ensure the success of a particular bill.

The Specific Contribution of Social Work and the Social Reformers

The contribution of social work in furthering progressive Social Security changes has already been referred to in considering the role of the American Association of Social Workers. This professional organization of persons in public and private social work, was the main channel for communicating social workers' thinking and stance on policy issues. There were also organizations like the American Public Welfare Association, the National Social Welfare Assembly and the National Federation of Settlements and Neighborhood Centers, representing other social welfare personnel, that spoke on policy issues of particular concern and interest to them.

A basic question that has to be dealt with in discussing the role of social work and social workers is the definition of the term "social worker." Indeed this is questioned even today, when the social workers' role in influencing social policy changes is debated. Is "social worker" to be restricted to those who are professionally educated in social work at the Master's degree level and are members of the professional association? Is it also to include those not professionally "qualified" but knowledgeable and competent in the area of social welfare, including social insurance? And, in applying whatever insights this study can provide for social welfare workers today, how should we classify the growing category of paraprofessionals? The answers to these questions are important in considering the extent to which social workers were then or, for that matter, are now exercising any kind of influence in the social policy area.

If the broader view is taken—of including individuals knowledgeable and competent in the area of social welfare, but not necessarily professionally qualified—then reference could be made to the significant contributions from 1935 to 1954 made by persons of the caliber of Eveline Burns, Wilbur Cohen, Arthur Altmeyer and Elizabeth Wickenden, to mention only a few. Indeed, it was this broader interpretation that made possible the election of Arthur Altmeyer as

the President of the National Conference of Social Work in 1954. However, it should be noted that even today there are thoughtful persons within the profession who would want to restrict the term to those professionally qualified.

It is certainly possible to include also persons with competence and interest in the broad area of social welfare, not necessarily professionally qualified but active in areas of social policy and institutional change, in the category of social reformers. Reference has been made to social reformers as persons who played an effective role in bringing about changes in social policy and social institutions and in advancing social programs. They could be associated with government programs or private organizations and, while some social reformers made their contribution mainly through application of their thinking, others concentrated equally on rallying supporters for their cause.

There were also social workers who, because of their wider interests, work experience or knowledge base, were being drawn into the area of social reform and policy. They collaborated with social reformers in pushing for Social Security changes. Perhaps this collaboration was not a conscious and organized effort, but nevertheless it was significant. There emerged a nucleus of persons consisting of social workers and social reformers who gave considerable leadership to the social insurance movement.

Professional social workers, however, did not have as much experience in social insurance matters as in public assistance and relief work. Consequently, although they had played an active part in shaping FERA programs in the early 1930's, they were not equally active in the area of social insurance programs and policies. However, insofar as public assistance and social insurance were interrelated, social workers were drawn increasingly into the orbit of social insurance program and policy changes which were proposed. In 1954, for example, the AASW Committee on Public Social Policy agreed that the Association should center its major legislative interest in the field of Social Security, and, in particular, the OASI programs.

However, when social workers' efforts are compared with those of other reform movements (labor, above all), it will be evident that social workers lacked the necessary zeal or strength to influence social policy changes, even in the 1950's. Social workers' contributions were in providing expertise in certain areas, up and down the line in federal, state and local agencies. They also provided valuable feedbacks, on the basis of experience, for implementing programs, and focused considerable attention, primarily through educational efforts, on major policy issues such as the merit principle, extension of coverage to new groups and provisions for disability insurance. In situations where they worked in cooperation with other groups—labor in particular—to push collectively for specific policy changes in areas in which they had competence (such as the merit principle issue prior to the 1939 amendments), they seemed to be more effective. The Social Security Board, its advisory councils and task forces served as a rallying point and facilitated collaboration among social workers, social reformers and other interest groups.

There were a few social reformers who were close to the social work profession and, together with social workers interested in progressive Social Security policies, they constituted an influential nucleus which included Harry Hopkins, Frances Perkins, Grace Abbott, Edith Abbott, Paul Kellogg, Douglas Brown, Eveline Burns, Abraham Epstein, Arthur Altmeyer, Wilbur Cohen and Elizabeth Wickenden. An appreciable part of the development of the original Act can be attributed to Frances Perkins, Harry Hopkins and Arthur Altmeyer, who worked closely with President Roosevelt. Altmeyer, as SSB Chairman, gravitated naturally into a strong leadership position because he had helped to originate the Act and to administer it from its "first official breath."

The Abbott sisters made their valuable contribution especially in the early part of the period under study. In 1936, for example, when Social Security was made an election issue by Governor Landon by his partisan attack on the Act, Grace Abbott in a nationwide radio address refuted his criticisms. Her address was made under the auspices of the Progressive National Committee and labor's Non-Par-

tisan League supporting Franklin D. Roosevelt for president. Grace Abbott was a member of PNC supporting Roosevelt's candidacy, but she spoke primarily as a social work leader. "As a social worker," she said, she was aware of the hardships faced by the elderly in the absence of Social Security protection. "Any student of the social reform movement," she argued, would know that Governor Landon's proposals would lead to "poor relief" and a return to the principles of Elizabethan poor laws. [29] This was but one example of the manner in which members of this nucleus of social reformers and social workers spoke out for progressive Social Security policies and countered the often unfounded attacks on Social Security.

Eveline Burns likewise, played a key role in several ways: in offering effective criticism of the Chamber of Commerce Social Security proposals [30]; in participating as a member of special committees and task forces; and in testifying before Congressional committees in favor of progressive Social Security policies. Others such as Paul Kellogg and Douglas Brown made their own unique contributions. Wilbur Cohen from within the administration proved to be an able negotiator in dealing with reform groups, and influential with Congress. He handled the negotiations leading to the policy changes for each of the amendments, except the 1954 amendments.

In the context of the leadership roles exercised by this core group of social reformers and social workers, there has been the argument that underlying much of Social Security development has been "happenstance of personalities." What would have happened, it is asked, if there had not been a President Roosevelt to give effective leadership, or a Frances Perkins, Harry Hopkins or Arthur Altmeyer? Without diminishing in the slightest the unique contributions of these individual men and women, we must remind ourselves that social policy changes are synthesized historically from the interaction of several forces, of which the role and the influence of brilliant personalities is but one. In another socio-economic milieu—a period of prosperity, for example—little heed likely would have been given these humane and creative leaders.

We have already reviewed the distinctive roles and emphases of

each of the major reform movements upon which these leaders relied so heavily. We have seen how each group's activities were conditioned by its origins, composition, goals, priorities and resources. Some of them, in the crucible of working in behalf of Social Security advancement, gained much in political maturity and in sophistication regarding tactics and strategies, in many cases new to them.

Several reform movements acquired expertise in the use of adverse criticism and controversy, refuting unfounded attacks by making accurate information available at the strategic time and place; in the mobilization of beneficiaries or affected groups themselves (e.g., the aged, the farm workers); in collaboration with other groups on specific issues; and in neutralizing or limiting opposing forces. Another tactic used by some reform movements in supporting Social Security concepts and programs was to show how the concepts and programs were harmonious with traditional values and social patterns, such as self-help, insurance, and mutual aid—all of which were inherent in the Social Security program. This was particularly effective in counteracting the resistance of conservative forces. In the wise use of traditional ideas and motivations to support such significant change, the Social Security policies and programs that have emerged are a remarkable example of the success of "a planned and deliberate effort to bring about a major and permanent social reform." [31] However, we should exert sound judgment in appealing to tradition within every new context, knowing that traditional values are not automatically and universally applicable; that traditional motivations, concepts and values must often be acknowledged as impediments to individual and social growth, particularly when we strive toward a great leap in our evolution. But the social reformers who created and nurtured our Social Security program could use the appeal to tradition ethically, pragmatically and persuasively.

In historical perspective, the role of the nucleus of social workers and social reformers committed to policy changes in social insurance was certainly unique. So, too, was the role of the reform groups,

individually and collectively. The question remains to plague us as to how much weight can be attached to the role of each—the core group of individual leaders and the reform organizations—in the framework of events and socio-economic conditions that cried out for change. No study, no available data, and no set of research controls can permit exact assessments of this type. Undoubtedly, however, one can safely conclude that the unique personalities and the reform movements were, deliberately or not, indivisible in the shaping of this aspect of our social history.

NOTES

1. "Social Security and the Townsend Plan," *The American Forum of the Air*. Vol. 2, No. 21, Ransdell, Inc., Washington, D.C., 1940.

2. See N. Viswanathan, *The Role of the American Public Welfare Association in the Formulation and Development of Public Welfare Policies in the U.S. 1930-1960*, Unpublished doctoral dissertation, New York School of Social Work, Columbia University, 1961.

3. Conference of Social Security Board Members with AASW Representatives 3/28/1938. American Association for Advancement of Science; *Records of the Chairman, Social Security Board 1935-1940*; National Archives, Record Group 47, Washington D. C.

4. James E. Marquis. "Old Age and Survivors' Insurance: Coverage Under the 1954 Amendments," *Social Security Bulletin*, Vol. 18, No. 1, January 1955, p. 5.

5. Abraham Holtzman, *op. cit.*, p. 104.

6. *Ibid.*, p. 87.

7. Interview by the author with Charles I. Schottland, Waltham, Mass., September 21, 1970.

8. Holtzman, *op. cit.*, pp. 125-126.

9. *Ibid.*, pp. 132-134.

10. *Ibid.*, p. 203

11. Citizens Conference on Social Security, News Release 5/13/1953, Social Security Amendments 1953, IV NN6, *National Consumers' League Papers*, Manuscripts Division, Library of Congress, Washington D.C.

12. See, for example, the memorandum to General Watson from Arthur J. Altmeyer on the AFL Committee on Social Security, 4/4/1941, President Roosevelt Correspondence 1941-1945, *Arthur J. Altmeyer Papers;* Manuscripts Library, State Historical Society of Wisconsin.

13. Committee on Social Security, AFL-CIO, AFL-CIO Social Security Committee, December 1955, *Nelson Cruikshank Papers*, Manuscripts Library, State Historical Society of Wisconsin, p. 3.

14. See Letter to President from Grace Abbott 3/15/1935, University of Chicago, *Records of the Chairman Social Security Board, 1935-1940*, National Archives, Record Group 47, Washington D.C.

15. Lubove, *op. cit.*, pp. 141-143 and pp. 173-174.

16. Corning, *op. cit.*, p. 42.

17. For an analysis of the role of the Social Security Board in formulation and development of policy in a related area, see Saiyid Zafar Hasan, *Policy Formulation and Development in Public Assistance: A Study of the Role of the Federal Government in the First Five Years of the Social Security Act 1935-1940*, Unpublished doctoral dissertation, New York School of Social Work, Columbia University, 1958.

18. Labor Information Service, Social Security Board, Correspondence Social Security Board, File B—Social Security File, *American Federation of Labor Papers*, Manuscripts Library, State Historical Society of Wisconsin.

19. Letter of Mathew Woll, Chairman, AFL Committee on Social Security, to Arthur Altmeyer, Chairman, Social Security Board 10/30/1939; *Records of the Chairman, Social Security Board 1935-1940*, National Archives, Record Group 47, Washington, D.C. See also: CIO Social Security Committee Conference with Social Security Board 4/15/1942; Social Security Committee 1940-1942, *CIO Secretary-Treasurer's Office Collection*, Wayne State University Labor History and Urban Affairs Archives.

20. *The CIO News*, August 13, 1938.

21. Report of Social Security Committee, Minutes of Women's Joint Congressional Committee, 4/4/1949; Minutes 1949, Box 8, *Women's Joint Congressional Committee Papers*, Manuscripts Division, Library of Congress, Washington D. C.

22. Committee on Social Security, AFL-CIO, *op. cit.*, p. 2.

23. Clipping from the Providence, Rhode Island Journal, File 011.3 Protest, Opposition and Criticism, *Records of the Chairman, Social Security Board 1935-1940*, National Archives, Record Group 47, Washington, D.C.

24. *New York Times*, December 22, 1934.

25. Letter from Robert Huse to Frank Bane 8/3/1938, File 011.4, Resolution and Recommendation, *Records of the Chairman, Social Security Board 1935-1940*, National Archives, Record Group 47, Washington, D.C.

26. Letter from Lamar Tooze, President, Portland League of Women Voters, to Constance Roach, 2/4/1936, FG 164 Box 344, *League of Women Voters Papers*, Manuscripts Division, Library of Congress, Washington, D.C.

27. Memorandum of 5/16/1942, from Joseph Kovner to James B. Carey, Townsend National Recovery Plan, *CIO Secretary-Treasurer's Office Collection*, Wayne State University Labor History and Urban Affairs Archives.

28. *Townsend Weekly*, Vol. 19, No. 23, June 13, 1953.

29. Text of the radio address by Miss Grace Abbott, "Landon Would Take Us Back to the Age of Elizabeth," 9/29/1936, Progressive National Committee Supporting Franklin D. Roosevelt for President, New York.

30. Eveline Burns. "Comments on the Chamber of Commerce Social Security Proposals," Social Security Amendments 1953, IV NN6, *National Consumers' League Papers*, Manuscripts Division, Library of Congress, Washington, D.C.

31. Robert M. Ball, "Concluding Remarks," William G. Bowen, *et al.*, eds., *The American System of Social Insurance: Its Philosophy, Impact, and Future Development*. New York: McGraw-Hill Book Company, 1968, p. 241.

VI

Social Work's Challenge in the Years Ahead in Policy Formulation and Change

"America is promises," ... We have it in our power now to convert those promises into fulfillment. We have at our disposal all the material for such fulfillment. We know the techniques. It is no longer a question of ignorance or bewilderment. It has become quite simply a question of will and purpose and good faith. ...

If we miss this chance, we may not get another until the next Great Depression and the next World War. And this time the depression may not escape social violence. And this time the war may prove to be a War of Annihilation.

Bruce Bliven, *et al.*, "Charter for Americans," *The New Republic*, April 19, 1943.

181

Social Work and the Arena of Policy Process

THE TWENTIETH CENTURY is uniquely the era of "pervasive and persistent social change." The social work profession, which in a strict sense came into being in this century, faces the challenge of being increasingly responsive to the changes and the new needs that arise in society. What should be the profession's response? Specifically, how should the social work profession respond to the challenge of being involved in policy formulation and change? What are the issues that have to be dealt with in this task?

It is perhaps unrealistic to think that social workers by themselves could exercise a dominant change role, given the complexity of the policy process. However, social workers in collaboration with other strategic forces assuredly can play a more effective role.

There is undoubtedly a growing awareness of the need to enter the policy-making arena, to influence policy changes. [1] Increasingly, individual social workers are engaged in this task of policy formulation at different levels, often working in collaboration with persons from other disciplines. This is evident at the state and national level where social workers have to some extent in recent years begun to work close to the policy arena as policy analysts, consultants, legislative aides and planners, collaborating with members of allied disciplines. Individual social workers have also as citizens actively participated in citizen groups working toward specific policy changes. But what is the trend in the profession as a whole? While there is a great deal of interest and willingness to explore this often conflicting and confused area of policy formulation and change, there are certain barriers that seem to stand in the way.

Among the factors that impede involvement in the political process and policy decisions are the view that "politics is dirty"; the predominant emphasis in the profession on "*micro* rather than

macro changes"; the situation where the profession is often confused with the agency; and the "binding effects" of often being locked into the "social welfare bureaucracy." [2]

The extent to which social workers will be involved in the policy arena is also tied up with the outcome of the ongoing debate as to what extent the social work profession should focus on the developmental function in addition to remedial, preventive and supportive functions. The developmental function will necessitate close attention to goals and direction of social policy; development of resources, the basis for allocation of social and economic resources and their impact on people; and a more integrated approach in the development of social and economic policies. The international conference of ministers responsible for social welfare held under the auspices of the United Nations in 1968, for example, highlighted the urgent need for social workers to participate in and contribute to the development of policy and to consider the role of social welfare in the context of national development. [3]

It could be held that the political process is the major instrument for introducing social reform and significant social policy changes—noting at the same time that not all social policy is legislated and that a fair amount of social policy related to "persons in need" is not to be found in statutes. [4] The Social Security program introduced by the Act of 1935 and the progressive changes that followed are unique examples of the success of deliberately planned efforts to introduce major social policy changes through the legislative process. Major policy decisions regarding social welfare programs will likely continue to be made through the political process, and in some instances as a by-product of legislation designed for other purposes. In this context, the degree of commitment by the social work profession to enter this arena of policy process, and to consider relevant functions here as intimately related to social work practice seems crucial.

Needless to say, the decision to enter the arena of policy process does not imply the abandonment of the traditional tasks and concerns of the profession. Rather it should be seen as helping to

strengthen these very tasks in the effort to influence policies that determine the basis and the framework within which these tasks are performed, and new ones undertaken as necessary. It is a challenge to respond equally to the "priestly" and the "prophetic" aspects of the profession, to service as well as reform and policy changes. [5]

Some social workers have said that when the social worker attempts to influence policy formulation or change at levels beyond the client, the family and persons who have a direct interest or responsibility for the client's well-being, the situation becomes complex and efforts seem futile. In this context it has been stated that "to characterize as a responsibility of professional social work" the effecting of social policy changes at levels involving the lives of large masses of people is to minimize the "myriad forces, persons, values and aspirations" that operate in the policy-making process. [6] It is said that, as the scope of policy and the range of persons and institutions that it influences become more "inclusive," it becomes "unwieldy" for the social workers as well as others who are more directly involved in the policy process. However, the complex and conflicting nature of the policy process, and the fact that social workers as an "interest group" will be one of several other interest groups are insufficient arguments for abdicating responsibility in the policy-making arena. It is perhaps unrealistic for social workers to think that they could by themselves influence social policy. The other extreme, however, is to shy away from this important area of responsibility, stating that the process is too confused, that efforts amount to nothing very significant, that it is not even possible to know who makes social policy. [7] Indeed this very situation challenges the social work profession to respond with greater resourcefulness; special skills; research on policy process as to significant points at which strategic intervention is effective; flexibility in working with other groups; and the capacity to present the values and policy stands of social workers and related interests in competition with others.

Peter Rossi maintains that social workers should increasingly in the future move closer to the public sector of community life and

work closely with the politician. He speaks of the need for "Harry Hopkinses all over the country." "Social workers," he points out, "need the politician and he needs them." The entry of social workers into the public sector of community life in this way would lead ultimately to entry into similar capacities on state and national levels. In urging social workers to move closer to the politician, he suggests especially collaboration with politicians in the Democratic party, "whose commitment to the ideology of social welfare," he says, has "to be reinforced and given content." [8] While the identification of a professional group with one party may pose difficulties, the possibility of pushing for particular policy planks in party platforms, especially the Democratic party, the persistent efforts to see that they are implemented, and the mobilization of broad-based support for such policies constitute a real challenge.

It is clear that social workers, if they are to improve their effectiveness in the policy-making arena, must collaborate not only with the politicians who are in sympathy with the causes they espouse, but with other groups as well, notably consumer and client groups. In such collaboration a realistic understanding of the policy process and the obvious limits in any attempt to influence policy changes is essential. Social workers need to master new skills, especially those that will be necessary if the profession responds to the demand for emphasis on the developmental thrust. Included among them are skills in policy analysis, development of social indicators, evaluation of the impact of social and economic policies, interdisciplinary team effort, developmental planning, resource allocation, brokerage, advocacy, and the ability to organize/work with interest groups, low-income groups, and cultural and ethnic minority groups.

Perhaps, as has been suggested, social workers have to learn to be opportunists without betraying long-term goals. Are there ways of arriving at compromises without throwing social work values overboard? Could forces that are opposed or indifferent be used resourcefully? Policy agreements can bring together the strangest bedfellows—individuals of different ideological positions. It has, for instance, been suggested that the continuing support in Congress for

extension of OASI benefits arises from the desire of liberals to strengthen the welfare programs of the federal government and the desire of conservatives to minimize demands by unions for private pension plans. [9] In the effort to influence policy changes, the social work profession will have to work increasingly with varying interest groups and seek the kinds of compromises that make possible support for specific policies from groups with different interests and motivations.

New Directions in Social Work Education and Practice

In a sense the response of the profession to the challenge of policy formulation and change in the future will depend to an appreciable extent on the educational preparation of social workers. Much has happened since Eveline Burns and others focused attention on the need to give social policy an important place in the educational preparation of social workers, which calls for critical appraisal, questioning and assessment. [10] There is the need for an ongoing evaluation of professional educational objectives and the opportunity afforded for understanding and developing skills in policy formulation and change. Whom are we training? And for what? How do we see ourselves in relation to other professions, particularly in regard to planning and policy formulation? The social work profession will have to address itself to these and related questions in the effort to develop curricula that are relevant to the changes and newer demands made on the profession.

Increasingly, the social work profession will have to concentrate on preparing practitioners for responsibility in regard to the developmental function in addition to the customary remedial and preventive functions. This emphasis on the developmental function calls for newer emphases and changes in the curriculum. [11] Education for social work practice, in addition to ensuring competence in methods of working with people, will also have to emphasize competence in substantive areas related to policy, such as economic organization, political process, social justice, cultural and ethnic relations, and

demands of citizens' groups. In addition to the traditional social work concerns, the areas of resource development and allocation, integrative approach to social and economic policies, advocacy planning, developmental systems change and policy change—all will demand the most creative curricular thinking.

The developmental function, involving close ties with the policy process, and decisions regarding allocation of resources will necessitate educational preparation for greater competence in policy analysis, planning, evaluation of impact of policies, team effort, interdisciplinary collaboration, and work with political leaders and minority groups. Special competence will have to be developed in working with ethnic minorities and cultural groups, in understanding their aspirations, in developing policies that ensure greater justice to them, and in evaluating the impact of such policies.

The fact that the policy process is confused, that it is not always possible to determine who makes policy or "whom or what the social worker is supposed to influence" should not deter the profession, in its educational preparation, from making serious efforts to help the student to understand realistically the policy process, the conflicts, the compromise solutions that emerge and to equip them with a range of skills necessary for working in this area. It is to be seen as part of the general challenge in practically all fields of education today to focus on the discovery of the unknown, for coping with the situation of change and for developing a different sense of competence. [12]

Factors to Consider in Influencing Policy Changes

A brief attempt is made here to focus on some of the specific factors that social workers would seem to have to take into account increasingly in the future in efforts at policy changes, on the basis of insights provided by this study. Efforts at policy changes in some situations could, for example, be initiated at the local level and through state legislatures. There are those who maintain that the main effort by social work in introducing social reform or social

policy changes will be within the local community context. [13] State legislatures and governors could also be helpful in giving support to policies advocated at the national level.

The strategy of urging political parties to include specific policy planks in their party platforms could lend support to particular policies and facilitate further public debate and understanding. It is also important in this context to make use insofar as possible of forces favoring social reform as well as forces opposed to social reform. Forces opposed to social reform or particular policy changes may help to focus more on issues and public understanding of them by the controversies which they engender. Independent, nongovernmental forces have a vital contribution to make in introducing changes in policies and programs. We have seen, for example, how the Social Security Board's links with influential groups outside the Administration helped considerably in moving Social Security policies and programs forward.

The news media—the press, the television network, and the radio—are also important sources for influencing policy. The press can influence Congressmen by focusing on particular issues. The timing and the manner in which issues are presented seem crucial. Such devices as news releases, letters to the editor, and controversial articles and debates, to promote wider public interest and understanding on issues, should be exploited to the fullest.

There are also many ways in which social workers can affect legislators at both the national and state levels: personal contacts, written communications, transmitting resolutions of organizations and petitions signed by large numbers of persons. There could be meetings at strategic times between social workers and legislators to consider specific issues. Mass rallies and protest marches, carefully timed and planned, can have impact. Individual social workers may also support and work actively for legislators in their political campaigns. Writing to the President, making group representations, and sending petitions regarding particular issues—all have their important place.

In all this, the selection of appropriate strategies, the keeping of

alternative courses open, and the timing of action are crucial for success. What is needed most are an alliance of interest groups that will help to achieve the goals pursued, and a realistic acceptance of the fact that goals may not be attained *in toto*, that compromises may be necessary.

A further factor that the social work profession, along with other groups, has to consider in the efforts to influence policy decisions, and to speak on behalf of the disenfranchised and the poor, is the extent to which the policy system as it operates today is open to new participants or groups. It is evident that large numbers of individuals who are not sufficiently organized or who do not have "institutionalized interests in policy outcomes" have, at best, a limited voice in the policy process. It seems vital that the policy system be made more "responsive" and "adaptable" to the needs and demands of such persons. [14]

In social policy a basic objective is to provide people with a greater degree of choice and participation. However, for the many who are poor and disenfranchised, the extent of independence and freedom of action extended as a right is still a "mirage." [15] New structures and mechanisms for broad-based participation will have to be developed to ensure that policy target groups have a voice in the shaping of that policy. Increasingly, the social work profession will have to concern itself with determining how and to what extent societal goals and policies contribute to social justice and equality. A related issue will be whether the main emphasis in social policy is to be social control or social change. These are basic and persistent issues to which the profession will have to address itself increasingly in the future in its efforts to influence social policy changes.

NOTES

1. Reference is made, for example, in *Community Organization Curriculum in Graduate Social Work Education: Report and Recommendations* (Arnold Gurin, New York; published by CSWE, 1970) of the need to prepare future practitioners for intervention in the policy area and the value of making intercultural comparisons in social policy. Likewise, a study undertaken in the

United Kingdom *Community Work and Social Change: A Report on Training* (London; Longman Group Ltd., 1970) comments on the significance of moves towards an integrative approach in social policy. National and international conferences in social welfare have also been focusing on the role of social workers in social policy change. The theme of the 1972 (XVIth) International Conference on Social Welfare held in The Hague, Netherlands, 1972, it will be noted, was "Developing Social Policy in Conditions of Rapid Change."

2. Alan D. Wade. "The Social Worker in the Political Process," *The Social Welfare Forum, 1966.* New York: Columbia University Press, p. 55.

3. United Nations. *Proceedings of the International Conference of Ministers Responsible for Social Welfare.* New York, 1969.

4. Charles S. Levy. "The Social Worker as Agent of Policy Change," *Social Case Work.* Vol. 51, No. 2, February, 1970, p. 105.

5. See Chambers, *op. cit.,* p. 264. See also: Clarke A. Chambers. "An Historical Perspective on Political Action vs. Individualized Treatment," *Current Issues in Social Work Seen in Historical Perspective,* CSWE, 1962.

6. See Levy, *op. cit.,* pp. 103-104.

7. Campbell, *op. cit.,* pp. 86-87.

8. Rossi, *op. cit.,* p. 368.

9. Lindblom, *op. cit.,* p. 219.

10. See Eveline M. Burns. "Social Policy: The Stepchild of the Curriculum," *Proceedings of Ninth Annual Program Meeting.* CSWE, New York, 1961, pp. 23-34. See also Gurin, *op. cit.*

11. See Herman D. Stein. "Social Welfare and Development: Education and Training for the Seventies," in *Social Work Education in the Seventies.* XVth Congress of Schools of Social Work, Manila, Philippines, IASSW, 1970. See also John B. Turner. "Education for Practice with Minorities," in *Social Work.* Vol. 17, No. 3, May 1972.

12. Louis Lowy. "Whither Social Work Education and Social Change?" *Journal of Education for Social Work,* CSWE Vol. 4, No. 1, New York; 1968, p. 32.

13. Rossi, *op. cit.,* p. 359.

14. Eidenberg and Morey, *op. cit.,* pp. 242-243.

15. Eyden, *op. cit.,* p. 83.

Bibliography

Books, Pamphlets and Reports

Adrian, Charles P., ed. *Social Science and Community Action.* East Lansing: Michigan State University, 1960.

Altmeyer, Arthur J. *The Formative Years of Social Security.* Madison: The University of Wisconsin Press, 1966.

Appelbaum, Richard P. *Theories of Social Change.* Chicago: Markham Publishing Company, 1970.

Bauer, Raymond A., ed. *Social Indicators.* Cambridge: The Massachusetts Institute of Technology Press, 1966.

————, and Gergen, Kenneth A., eds. *The Study of Policy Formation.* New York: The Free Press, 1968.

Becker, Carl L. *Freedom and Responsibility in the American Way of Life.* New York: Vintage Books, 1945.

Bernstein, Irving. *The Lean Years.* Baltimore: Penguin Books, 1966.

Beveridge, Sir William. *Social Insurance and Allied Services.* New York: The Macmillan Company, 1942.

Bortz, Abe. *Social Security Sources in Federal Records 1934-1950.* Washington D. C., U. S. Government Printing Office, 1969.

Bowen, William G., *et al.,* eds. *The American System of Social Insurance: Its Philosophy, Impact and Future Development.* New York: McGraw-Hill Book Company, 1968.

Bremner, Robert H. *From the Depths.* New York: New York University Press, 1956.

Brown, Josephine Chapin. *Public Relief 1929-1939.* New York: Henry Holt and Company, 1940.

Burns, Eveline M. *Social Security and Public Policy.* New York: McGraw-Hill Book Company, Inc., 1956.

————. *Security, Work, and Relief Policies.* Report of the Committee on Long-range Work and Relief Policies to the National Resources Planning Board. (Eveline M. Burns, Director of Research.) Washington, D.C.: U.S. Government Printing Office, 1942.

————. *The American Social Security System.* New York: Houghton Mifflin Company, The Riverside Press, 1951.

————. *The Social Security Act Amendments of 1950: An Appen-

dix to the American Social Security System. Boston: Houghton Mifflin, 1949.

Cameron, William Bruce. *Modern Social Movements: A Sociological Outline.* New York: Random House, 1966.

Cantril, Hadley. *The Psychology of Social Movements.* New York: John Wiley and Sons, Inc., 1967.

Carlson, Valdemar. *Economic Security in the United States.* New York: McGraw-Hill Book Company, Inc., 1962.

Chambers, Clarke A. *Seedtime of Reform.* Ann Arbor: The University of Michigan Press, 1967.

Chapin, Stuart F., and Queen, Stuart A. *Research Memorandum on Social Work in the Depression.* New York: Social Science Research Council, 1937.

Coll, Blanche D. *Perspectives in Public Welfare.* Washington, D.C.: U.S. Government Printing Office, 1970.

Committee on Economic Security. *Report to the President.* Washington, D.C.: U.S. Government Printing Office, 1935.

—————. *Social Security in America: The Factual Background of the Social Security Act* as summarized from Staff Reports to the Committee . . . Published for the Committee . . . by the Social Security Board. Washington D.C., U.S. Government Printing Office, 1937.

Community Work and Social Change: A Report on Training. London: Longman Group Ltd., 1970.

Conkin, Paul K. *The New Deal.* New York: Thomas Y. Crowell Company, 1969.

Consultants on Social Security. *A Report to the Secretary of Health, Education, and Welfare on Extension of Old-Age and Survivors' Insurance to Additional Groups of Current Workers.* Washington, D.C.: U.S. Government Printing Office, 1954.

Corning, Peter A. *The Evolution of Medicare.* Research Report No. 29. Washington, D.C.: U.S. Government Printing Office, 1969.

Council on Social Work Education. *Current Issues in Social Work Seen in Historical Perspective,* 1962.

Cox, Fred M., *et al. Strategies of Community Organization: A Book of Readings.* Itasca, Ill.: F. E. Peacock Publishers, Inc., 1970.

Dahl, Robert A. *Modern Political Analysis.* Englewood Cliffs, N.J.: Prentice-Hall, Inc., 1963.

Degler, Carl N., ed. *The New Deal.* Chicago: Quadrangle Books, 1970.

De Schweinitz, Karl. *England's Road to Social Security.* New York: A. S. Barnes & Company, Inc., 1961.

—————. *People and Process in Social Security.* Washington, D.C.; American Council on Education, 1948.

Developing Social Policy in Conditions of Dynamic Change. U.S. Committee Report. XVIth International Conference on Social Welfare, The Hague, 1972.

Donnison, D. V., *et al. Social Policy and Administration: Studies in the Development of Social Services at the Local Level.* London: George Allen & Unwin, Ltd., 1967.

Ecklein, Joan L., and Lauffer, Armand. *Community Organizers and Social Planners.* New York: CSWE and John Wiley and Sons, Inc., 1972.

Eidenberg, Eugene, and Morey, Roy D. *An Act of Congress: The Legislative Process and the Making of Education Policy.* New York: W. W. Norton & Company, Inc., 1969.

Epstein, Abraham. *Insecurity: A Challenge to America.* New York: Random House, 1938.

Etzioni, Amitai. *Studies in Social Change.* New York: Holt, Rinehart and Winston, Inc., 1966.

—————, ed. *Readings on Modern Organizations.* Englewood Cliffs, N.J.: Prentice-Hall, Inc., 1969.

Eyden, Joan L. M. *Social Policy in Action.* London: Routledge and Kegan Paul, 1969.

Federal Emergency Relief Administration. *Unemployment Relief Census, 1933.* Washington, D.C.: U.S. Government Printing Office, 1934.

Freeman, Howard E., and Sherwood, Clarence C. *Social Research and Social Policy.* Englewood Cliffs, N.J.: Prentice-Hall, Inc., 1970.

Freidel, Frank. *The New Deal and the American People.* Englewood Cliffs, N.J.: Prentice-Hall, Inc., 1964.

Gagliardo, Domenico. *American Social Insurance.* New York: Harper & Brothers Publishers, 1955.

Gans, Herbert J. *People and Plans: Essays on Urban Problems and Solutions.* New York: Basic Books, 1968.

Goodman, Leonard H., ed. *Economic Progress and Social Welfare.* NASW. New York: Columbia University Press, 1966.

Gordon, Margaret E. *The Economics of Welfare Policy.* New York: Columbia University Press, 1963.

Greer, Thomas H. *American Social Reform Movements.* New York: Prentice-Hall, 1949.

Gurin, Arnold. *Community Organization, Curriculum in Graduate*

Social Work Education. New York: Council on Social Work Education, 1970.

————, and Perlman, Robert. *Community Organization and Social Planning.* New York: CSWE and John Wiley & Sons, Inc., 1972.

Haber, William, and Cohen, Wilbur J., eds. *Readings in Social Security.* New York: Prentice-Hall, Inc., 1948.

————. *Social Security: Programs, Problems and Policies.* Homewood, Ill.: Richard E. Irwin, Inc., 1960.

Hall, Penelope M. *The Social Services of Modern England.* London: Routledge and Kegan Paul, Ltd., 1963.

Hawley, Willis D., and Wirt, Frederick M., eds. *The Search for Community Power.* Englewood Cliffs, N.J.: Prentice-Hall, Inc., 1968.

Hofstadter, Richard. *Social Darwinism in American Thought.* Boston: Beacon Press, 1967.

————. *The Age of Reform.* New York: Random House, Vintage Books, 1955.

Hogan, John D., and Ianni, Francis A. J. *American Social Legislation.* New York: Harper & Brothers, 1956.

Holtzman, Abraham. *The Townsend Movement: A Political Study.* New York: Bookman Associates, Inc., 1963.

Inkeles, Alex. *Readings on Modern Sociology.* Englewood Cliffs, N.J.: Prentice-Hall, Inc., 1966.

Jacob, Charles E. *Policy and Bureaucracy.* New York: D. Van Nostrand Company, Inc., 1966.

Jenkins, Shirley, ed. *Social Security in International Perspective.* (Social Work and Social Issues Series) New York: Columbia University Press, 1969.

Kahn, Alfred J. *Studies in Social Policy and Planning.* New York: Russell Sage Foundation, 1969.

————. *Theory and Practice of Social Planning.* New York: Russell Sage Foundation, 1969.

Kassalow, Everett, ed. *The Role of Social Security in Economic Development.* Research Report No. 27. Office of Research and Statistics, Social Security Administration, Washington, D.C., U.S. Government Printing Office, 1968.

Keller, Morton, ed. *The New Deal.* New York: Holt, Rinehart and Winston, 1963.

Kershaw, Joseph A. *Government Against Poverty.* Chicago: Markham Publishing Company, 1970.

King, Wendell C. *Social Movements in the United States.* New York: Random House, 1965.

Klein, Philip. *From Philanthropy to Social Welfare.* San Francisco: Jossey-Bass, Inc., 1968.

Konopka, Gisela. *Eduard C. Lindeman and Social Work Philosophy.* Minneapolis: The University of Minnesota Press, 1958.

Kramer, Ralph M., and Specht, Harry, eds. *Readings in Community Organization Practice.* Englewood Cliffs, N.J.: Prentice-Hall, Inc., 1969.

Krinsky, Fred, and Boskin, Joseph. *The Welfare State: Who Is My Brother's Keeper?* Beverly Hills, Cal.: Glencoe Press, 1968.

Kuusi, Pekka. *Social Policy for the Sixties.* Helsinki: Finnish Social Policy Association, 1964.

Lampman, Robert J., ed. *Social Security Perspectives.* Madison: The University of Wisconsin Press, 1966.

Lerner, Daniel, and Lasswell, Harold D., eds. *The Policy Sciences.* Stanford: Stanford University Press, 1968.

Leuchtenberg, William E. *Franklin D. Roosevelt and the New Deal.* Harper and Row, 1965.

————, ed. *The New Deal: A Documentary History.* New York: Harper Torchbooks, 1968.

Lindblom, Charles E. *The Policy-Making Process.* Englewood Cliffs, N.J.: Prentice-Hall, Inc., 1968.

Litwack, Leon. *The American Labor Movement.* Englewood Cliffs, N.J.: Prentice-Hall, Inc., 1962.

Livingstone, Arthur. *Social Policy in Developing Countries.* New York: Humanities Press, 1969.

Lubove, Roy. *The Struggle for Social Security, 1900-1935.* Cambridge, Mass.: Harvard University Press, 1968.

Marris, Peter, and Rein, Martin. *Dilemmas of Social Reform: Poverty and Community Action in the United States.* New York: Atherton Press, 1967.

Marsh, David C. *The Future of the Welfare State.* Baltimore: Penguin Books, 1964.

Marshall, T. H. *Social Policy.* London: Hutchinson University Library, 1967.

Mayer, Robert. *Social Planning and Social Change.* Englewood Cliffs, N.J.: Prentice-Hall, Inc., 1972.

McLaughlin, Barry, ed. *Studies in Social Movements: A Psychological Perspective.* New York: The Free Press, 1969.

Morgan, James N., *et al. Income and Welfare in the United States.* New York: McGraw-Hill Book Company, Inc., 1962.

Morgan, John S., ed. *Welfare and Wisdom.* Toronto: University of Toronto Press, 1966.

Morris, Robert, ed. *Centrally Planned Change; Prospects and Concepts.* New York: National Association of Social Workers, 1964.
————, and Binstock, Robert H. *Feasible Planning for Social Change.* New York: Columbia University Press, 1966.
Munts, Raymond. *Bargaining for Health: Labor Unions, Health Insurance and Medical Care.* Madison: The University of Wisconsin Press, 1967.
National Association of Social Workers. *Changing Services for Changing Clients.* New York: Columbia University Press, 1969.
Niehoff, Arthur H., ed. *A Casebook of Social Change.* Chicago: Aldine Publishing Company, 1966.
Nisbet, Robert A. *Social Change and History.* New York: Oxford University Press, 1969.
Nordskog, John Eric. *Contemporary Social Reform Movements.* New York: Charles Scribner's Sons, 1954.
Political Science Quarterly. Special Issue: "The Future of Social Services." Vol. 40, No. 1, January-March 1969.
President's Research Committee on Social Trends. *Recent Social Trends in the United States.* Vols. I & II. New York: McGraw-Hill Book Company, 1933.
Proceedings of the International Conference of Ministers Responsible for Social Welfare. E. 69, IV. 4. New York: United Nations, 1969.
Proposed Changes in the Social Security Act: 1939, Washington, D.C., U.S. Government Printing Office, 1939.

Pumphrey, Ralph and Muriel, eds. *The Heritage of American Social Work.* New York: Columbia University Press, 1964.
Rayback, Joseph G. *A History of American Labor.* New York: The Free Press, 1966.
Rein, Martin. *Social Policy: Issues of Choice and Change.* New York: Random House, 1970.
Richardson, Henry J. *Economic and Financial Aspects of Social Security.* Toronto: University of Toronto Press, 1960.
Roamsco, Albert U. *The Poverty of Abundance: Hoover, the Nation, the Depression.* London: Oxford University Press, 1965.
Rose, Arnold. *The Power Structure: Political Process in American Society.* New York: Oxford University Press, 1967.
Rubinow, I. M. *Social Insurance.* New York: Henry, Holt and Co., 1913.
Schlesinger, Arthur M. *The Coming of the New Deal.* Boston: Houghton Mifflin Company, 1958.

Schorr, Alvin L. *Explorations in Social Policy*. New York: Basic Books, Inc., 1968.

Schottland, Charles I. *The Social Security Program in the United States*. New York: Appleton-Century-Crofts, 1963.

————, ed. *The Welfare State*. New York: Harper Torchbooks, 1967.

Sellin, Thorsten, ed. "Appraising the Social Security Program," *The Annals*, Vol. 202, March 1939.

Shonfield, Andrew, and Shaw, Stella, eds. *Social Indicators and Social Policy*. London: Heinemann Educational Books, 1972.

Simey, T. S. *Social Science and Social Purpose*. New York: Schocken Books, 1969.

Social Science Research Council. A Report of the Committee on Historiography. Bulletin 64, *The Social Sciences in Historical Study*. New York: Social Science Research Council, 1954.

Social Security in the United States, 1937. New York: American Association for Social Security, Inc., 1937.

Social Work Education in the Seventies: XVth Congress of Schools of Social Work, Manila, Philippines. International Association of Schools of Social Work, 1970.

Somers, Gerald G., ed. *Labor, Management and Social Policy*. Madison: The University of Wisconsin Press, 1963.

Steiner, Gilbert Y. *Social Insecurity: The Politics of Welfare*. Chicago: Rand McNally & Company, 1966.

Titmuss, Richard M. *Commitment to Welfare*. New York: Pantheon Books, 1968.

————. *Problems of Social Policy*. London: His Majesty's Stationery Office and Longmans, Green & Co., 1950.

————. *Essays on the Welfare State*. 2d ed. London: Unwin University Books, 1963.

————. *The Gift Relationship*. New York: Pantheon Books, Inc., 1971.

Townsend Weekly. Vol. 19, No. 23, June 13, 1953.

Training for Social Welfare: Fifth International Survey. E. 71, IV, 5. New York: United Nations, 1971.

Turner, John B., ed. *Neighborhood Organization for Community Action*. New York: National Association of Social Workers, 1968.

United Nations. *Proceedings of the International Conference of Ministers Responsible for Social Welfare*. New York, 1969.

U.S. Bureau of the Census. *Historical Statistics of the United States, Colonial Times to 1957*, Washington, D.C.: U.S. Government Printing Office, 1960.

U.S. Bureau of the Census. Social Security Administration. *Basic Readings in Social Security.* Washington D.C.: U.S. Government Printing Office, 1960.

U.S. Bureau of Foreign and Domestic Commerce. Statistical Abstract of the United States, 1934. Washington, D.C.: U.S. Government Printing Office, 1934.

U.S. Bureau of Foreign and Domestic Commerce. Statistical Abstract of the United States 1936, Washington, D.C.: U.S. Government Printing Office, 1936.

U.S. Congress. House. Committee on Ways and Means, *Social Security. Hearings Relative to the Social Security Act Amendments of 1939,* Vols. I & II. 76th Congress, 1st Session. Washington, D.C.: U.S. Government Printing Office, 1939.

————. House. Committee on Ways and Means. Social Security Technical Staff. *Issues in Social Security....* Washington, D.C.: U.S. Government Printing Office, 1946.

————. House. Committee on Ways and Means. *Amendments to Social Security Act. Hearings.... 79th Congress 2nd Session, on Social Security Legislation.* Vols. I & II. Washington, D.C.: U.S. Government Printing Office, 1946.

————. House. Committee on Ways and Means. *Amendments to Social Security Act. Hearings ... on H. R. 2892, 81st Congress, 1st Session.* Vols. I & II. Washington, D.C.: U.S. Government Printing Office, 1949.

————. House. Committee on Ways and Means. *Amendments to Social Security Act. Hearings ... on H. R. 2893, 81st Congress, 1st Session.* Vols. I & II. Washington, D.C.: U.S. Government Printing Office, 1949.

————. House. Committee on Ways and Means. *Social Security Act Amendments of 1952. (House Rept. 1944 on H. R. 7800, 82nd Congress, 2nd Session.)* Washington, D.C.: U.S. Government Printing Office, 1952.

————. House. Committee on Ways and Means. *Social Security Act Amendments of 1954. Hearings, 83rd Congress, 2nd Session, on H. R. 7199.* Washington, D.C.: U.S. Government Printing Office, 1954.

————. House. Committee on Ways and Means. *The Social Security Bill. (House Rept. 615 on H. R. 7260, 74th Congress, 1st Session.)* Washington, D.C.: U.S. Government Printing Office, 1935.

————. Senate. Advisory Council on Social Security. *Final Report ... December 10, 1938.* (Senate Dec. 4, 76th Congress, 1st

Session.) Washington, D.C.: U.S. Government Printing Office, 1939.

————. Senate. Committee on Finance. *Social Security Amendments of 1954. Hearings, 83rd Congress, 2nd Session, on H. R. 9366.* Washington, D.C.: U.S. Government Printing Office, 1954.

————. Senate. Committee on Finance. *Social Security Act Amendments. Hearings on H. R. 6635, 76th Congress, 1st Session.* Washington, D.C.: U.S. Government Printing Office, 1939.

————. Senate. Committee on Finance. *Social Security Act Amendments 1950. (Senate Rept. 1669 on H. R. 6000 81st Congress, 2nd Session)* Washington, D.C.: U.S. Government Printing Office, 1950.

U.S. Department of Health, Education and Welfare. *Social Security Anniversary–1968: A Third of a Century.* Washington, D.C.: U.S. Government Printing Office, 1968.

————. *Social Security in the United States.* Washington, D.C.: U.S. Government Printing Office, 1953.

————. *Social Security Programs in the United States.* Washington, D.C.: U.S. Government Printing Office, 1968.

————. *Toward a Social Report.* Washington, D.C.: U.S. Government Printing Office, 1969.

U.S. Social Security Board. *Proposed Changes in the Social Security Act: A Report of the Social Security Board to the President and Congress of the United States.* Washington, D.C.: U.S. Government Printing Office, 1939.

Webb, Eugene J., *et al. Unobtrusive Measures: Non-reactive Research in the Social Sciences.* Chicago: Rand-McNally & Co., 1966.

Weekly News Service. American Federation of Labor. Vol. 29, No. 25 (June 24, 1939).

Wilensky, Harold L., and Lebeaux, Charles N. *Industrial Society and Social Welfare.* New York: The Free Press, 1965.

Witte, Edwin E. *The Development of the Social Security Act.* Madison: The University of Wisconsin Press, 1963.

Wolfinger, Raymond E. *Readings in American Political Behavior.* Englewood Cliffs, N.J.: Prentice-Hall, Inc., 1966.

Articles, Essays, and Addresses

Altmeyer, Arthur J. "Ten Years of Social Security," *Survey Graphic.* Vol. XXXIV (September 1945).

Begeman, Jean. "The Plan for Social Security," *The New Republic* (April 27, 1953).

Brown, Douglas J. "Old-Age Insurance Under the Social Security Act," *National Municipal Review*. Vol. XXV. No. 3 (March 1936).

Burns, Eveline M. "Can Social Insurance Provide Social Security?" in *Social Security in the United States*. New York: American Association for Social Security, 1935.

——. "Social Policy: The Step-Child of the Curriculum," in *Education for Social Work: Proceedings of Ninth Annual Program Meeting*, Council on Social Work Education, New York: The Council, 1961.

——. "Social Security: Social Insurance in Evolution," *American Economic Review*. Vol. XXXIV, No. 1, Part 2 (March 1944).

Campbell, Alan K. "Decision-Makers in Social Policy," *The Social Welfare Forum, 1970*. New York: Columbia University Press, 1970.

"Charter for America," *The New Republic* (April 9, 1943).

Cohen, Wilbur J. "Aspects of Legislative History of the Social Security Act Amendments of 1950," *Industrial and Labor Relations Review*. Vol. 4, No. 2, (January 1951).

——. "Discussion: Some Issues and Goals in Social Security," Reprinted from *Industrial and Labor Relations Review*. Vol. 12, No. 4 (July 1959).

——. "What Every Social Worker Should Know About Political Action," *Social Work*. Vol. II, No. 3 (July 1966).

——, and Myers, Robert J., "Social Security Act Amendments of 1950: A Summary and Legislative History," *Social Security Bulletin* (October 1950).

Cruikshank, Nelson H. "H.R. 6000 and You," *The American Federationist* (October 1949).

——. "The Social Security Amendments of 1954," *The American Federationist* (September 1954).

Epstein, Abraham. "Social Security—Where Are We Now?" *Harper's Magazine* (June 1940)

——. "Our Social Insecurity Act," *Harper's Magazine* (December 1935).

——. "The Future of Social Security: Needed Amendments in the Present Law." *The New Republic* (January 27, 1937).

Falk, I. S., and Cohen, Wilbur J. "Social Security for Farm People," *Journal of Farm Economics*. Vol. XXVIII, No. 1 (February 1946).

Gil, David. "A Systematic Approach to Social Policy Analysis," *The Social Service Review*. Vol. 44, No. 4 (December 1970).

Hodson, William. "Current Problems of Government and Social Work," *The Compass* (March 1937).

Jones, Hugh R. "Social Policy: We, the People Must Act," *The Social Welfare Forum, 1968*. New York: Columbia University Press, 1966.

Kahn, Dorothy C. "Social Work in the Security Program: Administrative Integration of Social Work in a Social Security Program which Includes Social Insurance," *The Compass* (November 1943).

Kidneigh, John C. "The Welfare State: What Is It?" in *The Welfare State, Menace or Millenium?* Social Science Research Center, University of Minnesota, 1950.

Leibowitz, James E. "Old-Age and Survivors' Insurance: Coverage Under the 1950 Amendments," *Social Security Bulletin* (December 1950).

Levy, Charles S. "The Social Worker as Agent of Policy Change," *Social Casework*. Vol. 51, No. 2 (February 1970)

Lowy, Louis. "Whither Social Work Education and Social Change?" *Journal of Education for Social Work*, CSWE. Vol. 4, No. 1, New York, 1968.

Lindblom, Charles E. "The Science of 'Muddling Through,'" *Readings in American Political Behavior*. Raymond E. Wolfinger, ed. Englewood Cliffs, N.J.: Prentice-Hall, Inc., 1966.

Marquis, James E. "Old-Age and Survivors' Insurance: Coverage Under the 1954 Amendments," *Social Security Bulletin*, Vol. 18, No. 1 (January 1955).

MacRae, Robert H. "Social Work and Social Action," *Social Service Review*. Vol. X1, No. 1 (March 1966).

Mayer, Robert. "Social Change or Service Delivery," *Social Welfare Forum, 1970*. New York: Columbia University Press, 1970.

McCormick, Mary J. "Social Advocacy: A New Dimension in Social Work," *Social Casework*. Vol. 51, No. 1 (January 1970).

Meyers, Robert J. "Old-Age and Survivors' Insurance: History of the Benefit Formula," *Social Security Bulletin* (May 1955).

Moscrop, Martha. "The Social Worker Is an Agent of Change," *Canadian Welfare* (January-February 1968).

Moynihan, Daniel P. "The Professionalization of Reform," *The Public Interest*. No. 1 (Fall 1965).

Rossi, Peter H. "Power and Politics: A Road to Social Reform," *Social Science Review*. Vol. XXXV, No. 4 (December 1961).

Rothwell, Charles E. "Foreword," *The Policy Sciences*. Daniel Ler-

ner and Harold Lasswell, eds. Stanford: Stanford University Press, 1968.

Schneiderman, Leonard. "The Political Functions of Social Work Practice," *Public Welfare.* Vol. XXXVIII, No. 2 (April 1970).

Statement of Welfare Policy Committee. "Public Welfare Platform: Objectives for Public Welfare Legislature in 1949," APWA, 1949.

"Social Security and the Townsend Plan," *The American Forum of the Air,* Vol. 2, No. 21. Washington D.C.: Ransdell, Inc., 1940.

Tandy, Elizabeth C. "Comparability of Maternal Mortality Rates in the States and Certain Foreign Countries." *Children's Bureau Publication.* No. 229. U.S. Department of Labor, Washington, D.C.: U.S. Government Printing Office, 1935.

The New York Times. Text of Governor Landon's Milwaukee Address on Economic Security (September 27, 1936).

Titmuss, Richard M. "The Role of Redistribution in Social Policy," *Social Security Bulletin.* Vol. 28, No. 6 (June 1965).

Turner, John B. "Education for Practice with Minorities, *Social Work,* Vol. 17, No. 3. (May 1972).

U.S. Chamber of Commerce. News Release on "Citizens' Conference on Social Security." (May 15, 1953).

Wade, Alan D. "The Social Worker in the Political Process," *The Social Welfare Forum.* New York: Columbia University Press, 1966.

Witte, Edwin E. "Twenty Years of Social Security," *Social Security Bulletin* (October 1955).

Unpublished Studies

Altmeyer, Arthur M. "The Significance of Social Security," *William Hodson Memorial Lecture Series.* Minneapolis, November 26, 1946.

Abbot, Grace. "Landon Would Take Us Back to the Age of Elizabeth," *Text of the radio address given under the auspices of the Progressive National Committee and Labor's Non-Partisan League Supporting Franklin D. Roosevelt for President,* on September 29, 1936.

American Association of Social Workers. *A Social Policy for To-day,* May 1949.

————. *Public Social Policy Bulletin* (prepared by Elizabeth Wickenden, Consultant on Public Social Policy). No. 1, November, 1953.

————. *Public Social Policy Bulletin.* No. 2, January 1954.

APWA Committee on Welfare Policy, "Next Steps for Action in the Field of Federal Welfare Policy," 1951.

Becker, Harry. "Organized Labor and Social Security," paper presented at a symposium, *The Quest for Economic Security.* University of Michigan, August 2, 1950.

Cohen, Wilbur J. "Social Security, The First 35 Years," 1968.

————. "The Legislative History of the Social Security Act Amendments of 1952," *Social Security Administration HEW.* Washington, D.C., 1954.

Cruikshank, Nelson H. "Some Labor Views on the Social Security Program," a paper presented at the Annual Meeting of the Industrial Relations Research Association, Washington, D.C., December 1953.

Hasan, Saiyid Zafar. *Policy Formulation and Development in Public Assistance: A Study of the Role of the Federal Government in the First Five Years of the Social Security Act 1935-1940.* Unpublished doctoral dissertation, New York School of Social Work, Columbia University, 1959.

Kidneigh, John C. "Administration and Community Organization in Social Work, in *Readings in Social Work Administration,* John C. Kidneigh, ed. University of Minnesota (mimeo), 1970.

U.S. Department of Health, Education and Welfare; Social Security Administration, "Summary of the Old-Age and Survivors' Insurance System as Modified by the 1954 Amendments," August 1954.

Viswanathan, N. *The Role of the American Public Welfare Association in the Formulation and Development of Public Welfare Policies in U.S. 1930-1960.* Unpublished doctoral dissertation, New York School of Social Work, Columbia University, 1961.